CREATING

A

BEAUTIFUL

HOME

From Starting Fresh

to Freshening Up—

Inspiring Ideas to Help You

Turn Your House into a Warm

and Welcoming Home

ILLUSTRATIONS BY
STEPHEN FREEBURG

WILLIAM MORROW AND COMPANY, INC.
NEW YORK

CREATING

A

Beautiful

HOME

Alexandra
Stoddard

It is the policy of William Morrow and Company, Inc.,
and its imprints and affiliates, recognizing the importance
of preserving what has been written, to print the books
we publish on acid-free paper, and we exert our best efforts
to that end.

Stoddard, Alexandra.
  Creating a beautiful home : from starting fresh to
freshening up : inspiring ideas to help you turn your
house into a warm and welcoming home / Alexandra
Stoddard : illustrations by Stephen Freeburg.
    p. cm.
  ISBN 0-688-10934-9
  1. Interior decoration—Psychological aspects.
  I. Title.
  NK2113.S82 1992
  747'.01'9—dc20   92-26054
                    CIP

Printed in the United States of America

6 7 8 9 10

BOOK DESIGN BY MARYSARAH QUINN

To my family—
Peter, Alexandra, Brooke

For your unqualified love I thank you.
I love you more than ever before now
that I have found my home.

CONTENTS

Part 1: THE HOUSE THAT TELLS WHO *YOU* ARE

1: "The Abiding Place of the Affections"   3

2: Reconsiderations of My Thoughts over Twenty-five Years   9

3: Getting Started: Putting Yourself in Your Place   23

4: The Essential Elements of Home Design   53

Part 2: CREATING YOUR BEAUTIFUL HOME

5: Entrances   83

6: The Living Room   95

7: Dining Places   123

8: Kitchens   135

9: Family Spaces   155

10: The Study   163

11: Your Bedroom   173

12: Children's Rooms   189

13: Bathrooms   201

14: Exteriors   243

15: Living at Home   221

Acknowledgments   227

Part 1

THE HOUSE
THAT TELLS
WHO *YOU* ARE

Chapter 1

"THE ABIDING PLACE OF THE AFFECTIONS"

STONINGTON VILLAGE, CONNECTICUT
JULY 6, 1992

Today we are celebrating the third anniversary of owning our sweet house. Peter and I are sitting in the sun by the sea. He describes our Connecticut village as "a small finger of land surrounded by water pointed toward heaven." We have fallen in love with our house completely. We immediately sensed that the house was blessed. Church carpenters began putting the frame in place in 1775 for the rectory of the first Baptist minister called to this community; and after living in this dear old house for a few short years, we know for certain that the house is enchanted. We know the history of the people who have lived here; we feel their integrity, character, love of family, country and home. Our house is under some magic spell. It delights us, charms us, captivates us, fascinates us, and above all, it enraptures us. This house has become our friend, our home.

One evening, as we sat by a fire in our living room with our feet up on a comfortable ottoman, we let the room fill with the pink glow of the fire and one single candle. We spoke again to each other about the overwhelming feeling we have when we are here, the divine, spiritual, make-believe quality to our house that

Home is a communion of the spirit.
—Peter Megargee Brown

we feel but can't articulate. We know our moods are elevated as we cross the threshold and there is a transformation from reality to fantasy. And we have come to understand that in this house we are fulfilling our impossible dreams, and living our days in contentment and grace.

As an interior designer, I thought I had a pretty good idea about what constitutes a "home." I thought I knew what my clients were going through when I helped them with their houses. But it wasn't until we bought this house that I had a clue to the powerful emotions a house can arouse. I had lived in many beautiful houses. There had been my parents' houses; there had been rented apartments, including the co-op I've shared with Peter for eighteen years, but (as astonishing as it seems to me now) never one I could call my own. Suddenly, I was the client. Everything became deeper and more full of meaning. As a professional, I became more vulnerable, an authority whose knowledge was mirrored back to me personally. For the first time, I was making decisions for our family in an old house that has a soul.

This process of turning a wreck of a house into our abode and then transforming the physical reality into a dream of the ideal home has made me look at my life's work with a new focus, different now because I see things more existentially. How I see and experience this process is the truth about my home. I see everything as if for the first time. The way the light falls on my desk in the morning matters terribly to me. I do the dishes at different times of day, depending on when the light floods into the white porcelain sink, not when a meal is finished. For the first time in my life, I have the luxury of making discoveries about a house that may not be apparent upon first inspection but become clear naturally, in time. Only through actual daily living—the reality of how we use the house as opposed to its appearance—can we know for sure how we feel at home.

Throughout this book I will ask you many questions about your house or apartment so that you can make your own discoveries and find the answers that best distill your aesthetic, that

To express yourself at home is an act of courage, just like happiness.

best fit your own needs and the requirements of your family, and that suit the character and integrity of where you live. Creating my home and writing this book has been a satisfyingly interactive process that has helped me to continue to define my personal philosophy. Asking myself these very same questions has led me to the answers that have helped me turn my own house into a home. As I describe what Peter and I have done, and what we still intend to do, I hope that you will think about those questions—and arrive at your own answers.

Whether you live in your first house or a temporary place, *your* home—or mine—is finally an attitude and a mind-set you can create and live in and love everyday. In our homes we have the freedom to center around our own uniqueness and spirit and to be at one with the people we choose to live with and love. Here, we can emphasize all the things we value and be personally responsible for the consequences of our choices. I have thought, with deep concentration and humility, about what constitutes a home. As with most of us, it is human to want to give physical expression to that which we hold sacred, and to define ourselves—through light, color, and texture—by the spaces we inhabit, yet I have been in far more *houses* than homes, as I'm sure you have, too. And in part it is the errors in our designs for living that this book seeks to redress.

Here, together, we can discover the evolution of a house and how it becomes a home. You will reflect on your own aspirations and on what's real and unchanging in your life. Home gently and subtly forces you to face the reality of your unique qualities and to mold, contour, adapt, build, and change the things that don't support this truth.

We live in houses, and when they transcend into homes, they envelop our personality. Whatever is right and good about our lives, whatever is authentic and beautiful, will be reflected in the atmosphere as well as in the details that mirror our souls in meaningful, tangible, physical ways.

We draw our strength from home by contemplating what is

Beauty has divine attributes.

most important to us. The nesting instinct is among the strongest urges in mankind. Subconsciously, we all yearn for this. Without knowing I was ever going to fall in love with an old house that would one day become my home, I instinctively began to prepare for this dream. Without knowing where, when, how, or why, Peter and I bought a pine corner cupboard when there was no corner to put it in; we bought hooked rugs, art, furniture, objects, quilts, and memorabilia wherever our travels took us. At the time, our purchases seemed like folly. Yet I know now that even in the most simple and random acts of accumulation, we were defining ourselves and evolving. In my own case, I was simply starving for a home and, like saving for a bride's "hope chest," buying and acquiring and giving evidence to an urge so strong and inexorable that it could no longer be denied. Not only would I, at nearly fifty, buy and live in my first house, but in the process I would be drawn into the ultimate joy and realization of a lifetime.

Our homes are intensely and profoundly personal, universally experienced by all of us, but lived in very differently. Dictionaries speak of residences or habitations, of physical structures and spaces; and about havens or shelters of happiness and love.

Peter told me his thoughts: "For me, a home is identified by characters that a mere house does not have: a communion of spirit of fellowship around the hearth, eating and drinking in the privacy of family and friends, security of place, protection from the dangers and turmoils of the outside. At home, there is the assurance of tolerance of idiosyncrasies. Above all, home allows us the comforts to do what we please with whom we please, and when we please. All combined, home is the ultimate exhilaration of body and soul."

Each of us will have a different way to describe the message and meaning of home. My own definition is that it is a metaphysical and spiritual place, an outward expression of an inward journey. Home is a melody and trinity of mind, body, and spirit, and the essence of the character and heart of those whom we

Style requires inventing something original.

love and with whom we choose to share our intimate selves. A home is a compelling experience that goes far beyond the architecture, no matter how beautifully proportioned and gracious. It is the ultimate assimilation of life's opportunities, and requires far more than attractively decorated rooms, an efficiently run household, or polite behavior. Pure contentment is brought on by our visceral enjoyment of the total home experience—the pleasure we take in our physical surroundings; our sense of satisfaction in the work we did ourselves to bring about these results; and the feelings we have about ourselves and the people sharing our lives. For me, home is the coming together of my past memories and experiences, of my love for my children, husband, and friends; my love of nature and beauty; my love of life and belief in continuity; my optimism tangibly expressed in life-enhancing ways—room by room—and of the tender appreciation that no matter how much of myself I put into this home, I, like everyone on earth, am a temporary guest. We all have one chance and then it is too late. To make, while we can, our home a sacred place seems to me the greatest challenge and opportunity of a lifetime.

As I am creating a beautiful home with Peter, I feel uplifted by those of you who are doing the same for yourselves and your families. I hope that the energy, power, and light of well-lived lives can inspire each of us on our private paths. I wish you every joy as you and I, mysteriously, are in the flow of creating beautiful homes.

Chapter 2

RECONSIDERATIONS OF MY THOUGHTS OVER TWENTY-FIVE YEARS

I'VE CHANGED MY MIND

"To change one's mind under changed circumstances is true wisdom," wrote Robert Louis Stevenson; and indeed changing times and personal experience have radically reshaped my thinking about the decoration of houses in today's world. My professional attitudes have evolved and altered significantly over thirty years as an interior designer. My spiritual mentor and friend Bishop John Bowen Coburn tells me that at midlife I've entered the age of the wise. I speak from deeply lived experience. The home has been my life's work—my life's passion, as well as my means of making a living. And in the process, I've given more than casual thought to the customs, culture, and direction of my chosen profession.

The reason I ended up spending my life in other people's houses was by default. I became an avid gardener as a young girl, as my mother had been, and when I would go inside my friends' houses, I was struck by how often they were dark and gloomy, which dampened my spirit at an early age. Bringing in the light—that became my mission. I came to understand that I was happiest in the sunshine, playing with my flowers, fruits, and vegetables, inspired by the colors and patterns, the smells

Maybe I work out my needs for change on my clients. I'm perfectly happy with what I have. It functions and it's very pretty.
—Eleanor McMillen Brown

and the beauty of nature. Why, I reasoned, should people have to settle for darkness when they were inside their houses?

I was still a teenager when I decided to become an interior designer. I thought this was an ideal profession for me, and at that time, like teaching or nursing, one that was looked on as natural for a woman. After all, women were the nesters, the nurturers, and the homemakers. Men went out in the world, making their gray flannel–suited fortunes, leather briefcases in hand. As Elsie de Wolfe, America's first interior decorator, stated in her 1916 book, *The House in Good Taste*, "Man made the house: women went him one better and made it a home." Who can dispute that truth?

I'm romantic by nature, but classic by choice. These two roots nourish my style and my innovations.
—John F. Saladino

♏ EN AND WOMEN, EQUALLY, CREATE A HOME

The first important change in my thinking is that, given the reality of our lives today, a home is created by humans—not just men or women, but by us as individuals and partners. My husband, Peter, is a man with a highly defined aesthetic who loves his home and is extremely capable of creating beauty and style in his private life. There is no question that homemaking with Peter has been intensely enjoyable, and I know that our Connecticut cottage is far richer than what I could have accomplished without his contributing talent.

But while my Peter may be one in a million, in this regard he is one *among* millions. Men are in fact as sensitive and concerned about the home and how it feels to them as we are. From my experience working with over a thousand families, I've discovered that men are *eager* to decorate and participate fully in decisions that have to do with the way they live at home. They care deeply about their creature comforts and will always make time to add enjoyment to their lives at home. Times may change slowly, but when they do, the changes are irreversible—and how glad we should be! Indeed, we have to rethink stereotypical notions from the past that are irrelevant today, but that many people still suffer from.

Men are not only equally as interested in creating a beautiful home, and as capable of making informed decisions, but are also, I believe, searching for outlets of creative self-expression. It is up to each of us to encourage and support men to participate fully in all homemaking decisions, from the arrangement of furniture and the selection of colors to the hinge of a door and the selection of a faucet. It is a proven fact that the more we personally participate in something, the more meaningful it becomes. Peter and I painted the inside of our house together, for example, and discovered that when you scrape, sand, and caulk and then prime and paint a surface of wood, you become attached to it the way new parents do with their newborn: You bond together in creating and understanding and appreciation. You take pride in what you do because you know what went into it, and you also feel the exhilaration of shared accomplishment. After I fell off a ladder while washing the living room windows and seriously injured my knee (requiring surgery), Peter drew the line for me: no scaffolding. I obeyed; no scaffolding. I don't do electrical work and plumbing, but I've done other forms of heavy work around the house and have felt better for having done it.

Men have always been aesthetically inclined, just as women have always derived satisfaction from manual labor. (I remember in the late 1940s watching my mother single-handedly lay an oak floor in our farmhouse in upstate New York.) While sitting on a plane recently during a flight from San Francisco to Columbus, Ohio, I watched in fascination as an attractive male passenger opened up his briefcase. Instead of reaching into it for what I assumed would be some boring financial documents, to my surprise, he whipped out a Bargello-stitch needlework square, which he explained he was working on for his dining-room-chair seat cushions. The shades of blues and yellows reminded me of Claude Monet's dining room at Giverny. The man smiled. "My

Cultivate individuality.

wife and I went to his house last summer when we were vacationing in France, and we both loved the combination and tones. I colored our dining room in a similar scheme." A male friend of mine hand-hooked all the rugs in his house in Cape Cod; and a client in Chicago made a dollhouse for his children and fully decorated it to scale, making all the furniture, floor, and window treatments himself. Impressive—and intimidating—as these particular examples are, the fact is that men like to tinker and putter.

Most important, today women and men consider themselves equal partners in all aspects of their lives together. We may make separate contributions, but we both participate fully at home. We are all born of a woman's womb, but a woman can no longer claim the house as her territory at the exclusion of her male partner. Men have always helped women to live more beautifully, and are now free to add richness, texture, and charm to their homes that are appreciated by everyone.

It also seems reverse prejudice to exclude men from any aspect of homemaking. I have little respect for a man who doesn't know where the ironing board is or where the sewing box is; nor for a woman who can't find a screwdriver in the toolbox. Home provides an instinctive outlet for self-expression, not gender distinctions. The creativity and fun of working around a house are not diminished or increased because someone is male or female. Everything will be more enjoyable when the home improvements, the puttering and decorating, are shared.

When a man is encouraged to create, great style can emerge. One of my clients is divorced, and his bachelor house is by far the most attractive, warm, and charming of all the places he and his former wife had lived in. What suddenly popped out of this man? I've been a longtime friend of his, and before the divorce forced him to fend for himself, all the decorating was handled exclusively by his former wife. This time things were entirely different.

We were actually grateful his former wife ended up keeping

A great many people enjoy having taste, but too few of them really enjoy the things they have taste about.
— Russell Lynes

their house. He could have a fresh start. All the colors for his house came out of his garden. His walls were lacquered and shimmering with pale, pastel tints. The exuberant flowered chintz used in the living room was called "Joy" by the great French fabric designer and colorist Manuel Canovas. (Apparently, Canovas was inspired when he looked down from a terrace into a garden at the delicate shades of sweet peas.) Today, Peter and I have the same chintz in our New York bedroom. After seeing our friend Don's living room, we knew immediately that this would be right for us.

My point here is that once Don involved himself fully in the process of creating his home, something wonderful happened. His active participation gave him a kind of joy he'd never experienced before. His new home, filled with natural light and a color palette that complemented the hopefulness and expectation of his brand-new life, was diametrically different from the house he'd shared with his former wife: dark woods, shuttered window treatments, primary colors. When I questioned him about this, it became clear that in the course of that previous decoration, Don had never been consulted as to his preferences. Perhaps his former wife believed that to be her domain; perhaps she believed that by choosing traditionally "masculine" colors and design treatments, she would be pleasing him—as many wives do.

(A note about color here: The truth is that many men abhor those blacks, browns, and primary reds, those blues and yellows we think of as "boy's colors." Men *like* pink—and the range of gentle pastels that have been stereotyped as distinctly—and separately—"feminine." In my experience with hundreds of male clients, living singly but more often *not*, I know there is no reason why a house has to look like the woods, full of forest greens and red and brown earth tones, just because it is a house full of males. Men—and boys—appreciate sunsets and sunrises, gardens and grass, and the sunlight on water. We've seen men increasingly drawn to dress shirts, leisure clothing, and accessories of lemon

Efficiency and convenience alone don't bring joy; beauty is the mysterious element.

yellow, soft pink, pale blue, and minty green. Remember the baseball cards of their youth were packaged along with pink bubble gum!)

Today, women are no longer the sole homemakers. Our notions about the house are in a turn-around. In earlier generations, the woman ran the household. Now, we can no longer let gender interfere: Men and women must contribute synergistically to the process of creating a beautiful life at home. This is something that must be thought through carefully if we are going to feel the true satisfaction and pleasure of creating and *living in* a home together.

Decorating, like cooking, should open up the senses.

We all respond to the era in which we live. When we are rigid and lose sight of the changing times, it becomes self-defeating. Younger generations are already thinking in terms of "our" home. But for my mother's era, it was quite different: In and out of the home, in her public and personal lives, she was dictated to by my father. But the old ways no longer work. Women no longer ask permission to live full lives, to utilize all their talents. It is up to men and women to rethink the reality of their domestic lives so there can be a greater ease and harmony in the spirit in which things are done.

I have a few practical suggestions for women. Take your husband with you when you shop for furniture. Your and your spouse's time are equally important. Don't make assumptions that you can't back up by fact. He is not too busy. What good is it taking a girlfriend with you to visit the furniture store when *she's* not the person who will live with it? Discover things as a couple. Get excited together. Many stores are open evenings and weekends. There are times that you can set aside for these shared experiences.

Don't speak for your husband. I wonder if some men are afraid to speak up at home. Unless you choose to live alone at home, you are creating this situation together. I dread hearing, "He leaves everything up to me." Homes cannot be created single-handedly. Share in the decision-making.

While some men will be eager to join in, others will have to be encouraged, cajoled—or led. But you can involve the uninvolved man in the process of creating your home, even in subtle ways. You can use your "down time"—holidays, weekends, vacations—to stroll casually together through antique stores or to walk through country villages exploring local shops. You can attend garage or estate sales during afternoons following morning tennis and golf matches, or go to an evening auction before taking in a late movie or dinner. Play up to and around your spouse's hobbies: If he's a collector, encourage him to join you in the search for that special wall or table display for his trophies and treasures. Create opportunities to explore, define, and assess your tastes together: For example, the music he enjoys *tells* you something. The art that draws him in a museum or gallery informs you about his color, texture, and mood preferences. Discuss what makes him comfortable, happiest, most fully himself. Remember, there are decisions that he must make. It makes no sense to design a bedroom or study for a man who cannot feel comfortable in it, or to purchase a gorgeous chair in which he's meant to read the Sunday paper or to watch a football game, but which is ill-proportioned to his body contours. Again, style is one thing, but a home without comfort is no home at all.

To sum up, then, whenever we feel discouraged and wonder why things aren't always wonderful, think of all the things you can do together at home. Men are spending more time with their families now than ever before and want to take on some of the responsibilities they used to leave to women. Pick up on their needs and the household will feel ever so much more like a home. Remember when you were first in love and you did everything together? It didn't matter where you were or what you were doing; everything about it was made special because you were doing it together.

*Let your rooms
radiate your love
of living.*

DESIGN YOUR LIFE, NOT YOUR HOUSE

The second key change in my thinking about the home is that we should take charge of our own life designs. The houses or apartments we live in, in whatever combination of circumstances, must adapt to us individually, and to our family's changing needs and requirements. We must rethink whom our home is for and to respond honestly to this reality. As a design professional, I have come to be passionately interested in what people do at home, day to day, where they do it, and why. But if my designer colleagues continue to concentrate on the decoration of houses without fully grasping how their clients are *living* in these houses, they will cease to be useful. Interior designers and decorators must put their clients' lives first and the house second, in order to help their clients to feel more comfortable at home. If the rooms are arranged for their clients' individual use and convenience, if they accommodate their unique rituals, ceremonies, and celebrations as beautifully as is practical, then professionals can be of service.

My clients often tell me they will never move. They say, "This is it." Yet, we do move. Our lives change. Life will continue to play tricks on us, and we have to be prepared to make appropriate adjustments. A woman in Naples, Florida, whose husband became a missionary in India during World War II, described to me the special classes they attended to train for living simply. Her teacher told the class that no matter how primitive their new homes would be, and they would be plain, to remember that no room could be more beautiful than one that was flooded with light and filled with good books and flowers. As we move forward, we never know where our lives will lead us. My husband has never been a missionary in India, but I don't rule out anything. When Peter and I got married, he told me there would be

Ambience must be genuinely your own.

a lot of surprises, so I'm staying open to all possibilities. Houses, no matter how humble or grand, come and go and ultimately do not define us. Home is an attitude that has to do with love and caring, thoughtfulness, honesty, and authenticity. It is our lives, our families, and our souls that need to be housed. But if you seek contentment by continually decorating your house, it may forever elude you. I've seen people compulsively decorate and redecorate, which I think betrays a restlessness that tells me that person's *spirit* has not found a home. I've also seen the most compulsively *decorated* house, but have glimpsed no life *behind* the decorations.

Interesting people create interesting houses. By being *ourselves*, we can break through the limitations imposed by place and circumstance. It is the expression of *well-lived* lives that creates beautiful spirit and charm in a house, not the beautiful furnishings. I've seen the homeliest houses transformed into havens of affection and joy by fascinating, high-spirited people. An architecturally elegant, symmetrical structure doesn't automatically translate into a relaxing, comfortable atmosphere in which we want to spend time alone and share our love of life with others. It may actually impede it and cause discomfort and rigidity. There are people who feel superior because they have the wealth to have everything they want, but this condition doesn't make them finer individuals. Their display of financial success doesn't speak of their character, their spirituality, their philosophy, their altruism, their kindness and sweetness or generosity; nor does it create warm, cozy, and comfortable residences where people can feel fully at ease and be themselves.

So I now approach interior design from a reverse point of view: The interior lives of the individuals who *inhabit* a house or apartment are important, not the traditional, and still accepted, viewpoint that a house should be properly "decorated." What I mean by this is, 99 percent of us live in houses that were designed for someone else. But you can't decorate *their* house any more than you can live their lives. We are housing *our* lives now, and

Create rooms for endless pleasure and feelings of well-being.

that cannot be dictated by abstract principles that say that a living room must be a living room, a dining room must be used as a dining room, and that a Tudor house must be an exact replica of a sixteenth-century residence.

Think of the inside of your house as your soul and the outside architecture as something like your bone structure, your genetic inheritance. The shell of the house is only an introduction to who we are. It is inside where we express ourselves, filling space with the personally meaningful, beautiful, and symbolic that affirm our individuality. We have to *move in emotionally.* In order for designers to be truly helpful to their clients they must understand this essential truth.

I'm not embarrassed about my reversal in thinking about what constitutes home, nor about departing so radically from many of my professional colleagues (as well as my beloved mentor, Mrs. Eleanor McMillen Brown). It seems wrong to separate decorating from lifestyle. I've been inside houses all my life, and more than ever I'm appreciative of the fact that home is central to our feelings of fulfillment. It is the hub of the wheel that allows us to explore all facets of a full and meaningful life. Home is where we can have perfect freedom to become the person we choose to be. Because home is crucial to our well-being and happiness, we (designers and dwellers alike) have to be more personally accommodating to our needs and desires and not be so compulsive about decorating the four walls. The house doesn't need to be "decorated." It will take care of itself.

Some of us have had unpleasant experiences with "experts"—be they institutional authorities or self-styled specialists—who seek to inform, dictate, or control our every move to the point of intimidation. My own profession has not been innocent of such excesses. Yet decorating, when not approached as a natural extension of who you really are, can be harmful, especially when it becomes so enslaved to status and fashion that it becomes artificial. If more people would live their lives hon-

Your home is the result of your own experiences and knowledgeable personal tastes.

estly, putting the things they love around them, I believe Americans would be far less anxious and disappointed. The art of living in today's world requires us to reach inside ourselves and search for the answers. As long as your home, and the choices you make for it, work for you, who cares what anyone else thinks? How you choose to live is really no one else's business. In fact, the more eccentric, personally defined, and quirky it is, the better. "You can't do that" is something you don't have to hear in your home. You darn well can. It is this absence of confidence in our own abilities to make the right choices in our lives at home that causes unnecessary pain, expense, and unease. Have fun is one of the messages of this book. Don't force anything. Don't rush. Living is a process. Everything will flow together in good time.

PERFECTIONISM KEEPS YOU FROM YOUR GOALS

The third, and possibly the most important, change in my attitude over the past twenty-five years concerns perfection. Perfect. Think about that word. When something is perfect, it can't be improved upon. Perfection is sterile, cold, and unloving. Perfectionists may feel superior and self-satisfied, but they are on the wrong track. Perfectionists rate low on self-esteem because nothing they do, or create, ever meets their standards. To feel strong and confident of our identity as we go through our busy days — this is what we want. But we are all *people*, ordinary human beings. How then can we expect to have perfect rooms when people themselves are imperfect?

Perfection, in the final analysis, halts the creative process. It is the enemy of spontaneity and serendipity, surely two of the most glorious gifts of life. In my experience working all over the United States, I've found there is too much emphasis

We need to straighten out our standards, and to get rid of a lot of rubbish that we have accumulated.
—Gustav Stickley

Decorating, like life, is a process. You never make a definitive statement because you are always making changes.

on nit-picking neatness, on creating rooms that are nothing more than still lifes. But where is the living taking place? Living well is an earthy business. We may celebrate the daily moments of life when we throw an extra log on a roaring fire, light a scented candle, open a window, move a chair over to the light, and sip a glass of Chardonnay; prepare a snack, read the paper, or write a letter with a fountain pen; but the soot, the scratches, the crumbs, the ring on the table, the mess on the floor, the ink on the chintz, the wrinkles, the work—these are all part of the romance of everyday living. Perfection, on the other hand, chills the mystery and leaves us frozen in space. Perfectionists miss it all.

Perfectionists make me nervous. I consider myself someone who likes things done right, but a broken glass or a scratch doesn't send me into clinical depression. Anyone who knows me understands that I like to set things up nicely and then I like to go for it and live fully. A bed *can* be a beautiful still life—when not in use—but pillow cases do get wrinkled and, yes, ripped. My old pine writing desk has several ink stains on the surface, some from my own pens. Without these, my desk wouldn't have a soul. It is, in fact, in the untidiness and the clutter of our cozy messes that we make our presence felt—and that, after all, is what *homes* are all about.

Live first and then maintain is my motto. Create rooms you can live in, that express you intimately. Show me a room in constant use that doesn't evidence some wear and tear. Show me a cheerful house that doesn't have faded fabrics. If you've made your choices based on your worst fears, then you have chosen unwisely. Would you not select a blue chintz for a house by the water because blue fades in the sun? I don't think so. It is far more charming to have sun-drenched, sun-bleached chintz—as fabric designers themselves can tell you. Many custom houses now offer prefaded materials in order to obtain that relaxed, sweet feeling that once upon a time could not be bought. Why discard that fine old Aubusson rug, which has been handed down for several generations, just because it's showing signs of wear? Over time, of course, rugs naturally become thin in spots, but this only adds to their charm. Isn't it far more important to feel wonderful in these rooms than to design and decorate a perfect room we feel uncomfortable using?

I have read Zen and Taoism, which have further reinforced my changed awareness. When I first became a student of the decorative arts, perfection was what we were striving for in everything visual. Because designers are paid to create the finest quality, any flaw was completely unacceptable. My own philosophical voyage in this regard has taken me far from my spiritual and professional mentors. I now know that perfection (and its corollary, the fear of mistake, a theme I'll develop in the next chapter) goes against the natural currents of the way we live and is itself lifeless. In reality, there is nothing in the universe that is completely perfect or completely still. As Alan W. Watts writes in *The Spirit of Zen*, "It is only in the minds of men that such concepts have arisen, and it is just those concepts which, according to Taoism, are at the root of human misery. For man clings onto things in the vain hope that they may remain still and perfect; he does not reconcile himself to the fact of change."

Anything is possible with hard work.
—Eleanor McMillen Brown

*T*HREE MAJOR CHANGES IN MY THINKING

1. Men and women equally create a home.
2. Design your life, not your home.
3. Perfectionism keeps you from your goals.

These reversals in my thinking are interconnected, as all things are. Only when men and women become equal partners is it possible to transform a physical shelter into a home. Together, by sharing the mundane and the mystery, we can mutually become enlightened by a creative synergism. When we live fully moment by moment, our house will reflect our lives as a pure image that mirrors more our inward spirit than as an artificial backdrop. Perfection allows for little peace, grace, and fun.

Remember, as this book now turns from the theory to the process of creating your beautiful home, to stay loose as you go along. Remember that beginnings are always more exhilarating than endings. Remember to be in the flow of your life so you enjoy every stage, all the steps, all the progress. Don't wait to celebrate today because your house isn't "finished." Uncork a bottle of wine, clink your glasses, and enjoy the moment completely. A house or apartment will never be finished if it is a home. Living well is a creative process where you find meaning and beauty in the present moment. Creating a beautiful home is an attitude and a way to open up to all the possibilities available to us as we move through our lives. Our true home is inside each of us. Our houses are the outward expression of something we have already achieved. It is your love of life that transforms your house into your home. There are phases and stages in our houses as there are chapters in our personal growth and enlightenment. These cannot be rushed or faked. There is never a point where we reach our ideal because that would imply decay and death.

We will find ourselves in changed circumstances in the future. Change is our only foundation. If you move, you will be able to bring with you some of your favorite things. You will be able to put your personal stamp on the next place you call home.

Having experienced these three changes in my attitude, I feel more freedom and contentment with this concept of home and I hope you will also.

Let your house set the tone for your life!

Chapter 3

GETTING STARTED:
PUTTING YOURSELF
IN YOUR PLACE

IS THE HOUSE THE RIGHT HOUSE FOR YOU?

You can't put heart and soul into a house that doesn't suit you. When we married, Peter and I considered keeping his charming Federal house in Southport, Connecticut, which I had always loved visiting. Instead, we decided to sell it. He had lived a full life in that lovely house, but that chapter was closed. We needed to make a new life together that would not be imitative, but that would be uniquely ours. Houses take on strongly the personalities of their owners. How you feel about a house is all that matters. You don't have to rationalize the way you feel. But what you do have to consider are the practicalities of your life—and find the way to bring them into balance with your dreams.

YOU HAVE TO FALL IN LOVE

In my experience, real estate alone, no matter how beautiful and dignified, no matter how easily you may come upon it, can rarely bring you joy. You have to be able to put yourself inside it. It's as simple as that.

You have to live in a house and know its circulation in order to furnish it decently.
—Karl Lagerfeld

Joanna and her husband, Mark, were house-hunting on the Saturday before Thanksgiving. This time it was in a new community. They'd been looking for months and had already been everywhere else. The broker had shown them seven houses; and darkness was beginning to fall, along with a cold rain, when the broker drove them to the eighth. Joanna recalls looking up at the white clapboard house from the bottom of the drive and thinking she didn't even want to go in. The grounds lacked landscaping and the house itself was so austere that she shivered and thought about the house from the movie *Psycho*: cold and forbidding. She decided to go in anyway and get it over with fast — the last house on that day's itinerary. To her surprise, the moment Joanna stepped inside, she knew she had found her home. There was a graceful entrance hall, charmingly proportioned rooms, simple yet elegant moldings, a beautiful, newly renovated country kitchen, a children's playroom with windows on three sides, and out back, a big old shady maple tree with a family-sized tree swing hanging from a strong branch. "I knew the second I was inside we could make this ours, and so we have. One of my secret pleasures is that anyone looking at the house from the street would never dream of the miracles of light and proportion inside. It's my every fantasy."

I had the exact same reaction to our dear old house in Connecticut. The first time I saw it was a few minutes before noon, the weekend before my daughter Alexandra's graduation from college. We had driven up to spend the weekend with friends, but because we were early for our invited time, Peter and I walked arm-in-arm down the village street, brilliant sunlight reflecting off the water as sailing and fishing boats passed by. We spotted an ugly, taupe-colored house with a greenish-blue front door and a FOR SALE sign out front. This house looked forlorn, like an abandoned orphan. We crossed the street and peered through the old glass windows into the living room. My heart pounded as I saw the sunlight dappling on the original pine floor. We walked around the south side of the house, past a small

A house becomes a friend after you experience a fierce level of enjoyment in it.

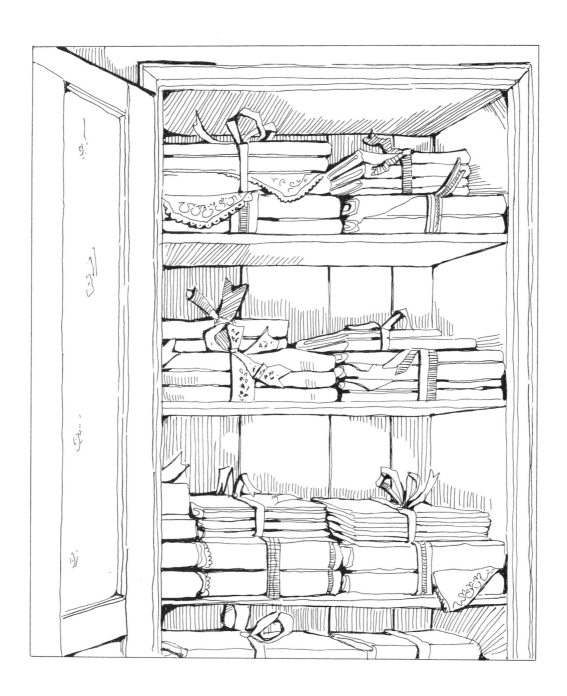

study, and we entered the "yard," a tiny patch of grass approximately the size of most of my clients' living room area rugs.

There, behind the house, were purple violets and white lilacs generously perfuming the area. In the yard next door, hugging a white picket fence (badly in need of a coat of paint), we discovered that our neighbor's tree was a purple lilac, while ours was white. The trees were intertwined in a hug of pleasure. Notice, I said "ours." This communion of lilac trees reminded me of the dogwood tree in my parents' backyard in Westport, Connecticut, where I grew up. A combination of pink and white had been grafted together to create this marriage of man and nature that brought great beauty.

It was love at first sight. Was it the lilac trees or was it the sweet disrepair of a house that reminded me of earlier days in Connecticut? Whatever it was, it didn't matter. By noon the next day we were inside the house, and by then, we were sure. This was it. We would buy our first house.

Like Joanna, I saw beyond the depressing colors, the peeling paint, the decrepit bathrooms, and the tarpaper hovel of a buttery. I felt the bones of the house instantly. Love is blind, and I fell in love unconditionally.

Two years later I would feel flushed with pride after meeting a distinguished elderly neighbor at a party. When we told the man that we were the couple who had bought the Reverend Rathbone's house, he laughed and congratulated us. "You have done a beautiful job fixing it up. I've lived here since 1920, and I don't believe I've ever seen an uglier house in New England. Come to think of it, I don't remember ever seeing an uglier house anywhere!"

The point I want to make here is that bringing a house back to glory (as we did) or finding the glory within (as Joanna is doing) is part of the bonding process, the transformation that takes place between you and your space (both inside and out). To the extent that we are able to make selections or choices that

*My business is to preach to you the beauty of suitability.
— Elsie de Wolfe*

satisfy ourselves and our needs, it is only a bonus when other people recognize what we did as worthy of praise. Spend your money on what makes you happy, not on what you can show off. Be authentic. Try to express yourself honestly in what you do. If we make choices based on what other people may think, we will be disappointed in life, because it won't be ours to live.

$\mathcal{D}$O WHAT SEEMS RIGHT FOR YOU

We find that when we express ourselves honestly and intimately we can feel confident about our choices. It is really our love and belief in what we are doing that give us the energy to create the transformation. Each of us is free to react and judge for ourselves. Peter and I fell in love with a house of Shaker simplicity that most people would find ill-equipped for modern living. There are exposed pipes and radiators throughout the house. There is no closet in our bedroom, and the bathroom is out in the hall, rooming-house style. The ceilings upstairs are 7 feet and 1 inch high—hardly majestic but adequate for us. The low ceilings help us save energy the same way they helped keep the rooms warm during the eighteenth-century winters. There is something inexplicably charming about the authenticity of its scale. We have learned to accept and work with our house's limitations.

Be responsible for the way your home looks and feels.

❖

$\mathcal{W}$E ARE DRAWN TO A HUMAN, HUMANE SCALE

We selected village life rather than rural life because it suited our temperaments. We have neighbors on all four sides, close to us. We hear laughter and babies crying, and we enjoy seeing activities all around us. We have no garage, which suits us too, because we have no car. The Fourth of July parade goes right by our picket fence. Neighbors wave. When in the village, we walk, ride our bikes, or get a lift.

Our dream was to find an eighteenth-century house in a quaint New England village with a view of the water. Big, open spaces aren't as comforting as rooms overlooking the water where we can sit by a fire and curl up with a book. When friends come over, we pull up chairs and the room proportions are ideal for warm, friendly conversation and laughter. The fact that I can stare at the fire and glance out at the water at the same time is unbelievably thrilling. But on a practical level, we needed to work on the plumbing; we needed a new furnace and boiler. Our roof was rotten. On a purely aesthetic level, the colors were dead Colonial—absorbing all light, depressingly somber. Everything in the house was in dire need of repair—not to mention that we would literally be decorating this place from the ground up.

TAKING ACTION— GETTING WHAT YOU REALLY WANT

We all want our home to be a true expression of ourselves. But too often we're timid about decorating because we have preconceived ideas of how a house *should* look. Inhibited by our lack of "expertise," we don't trust our ability to group furniture or select colors, and we worry that some of our possessions are a bit shabby or don't go together. And then there are those of us, starting out or starting over, who are eager to get going—but become so overwhelmed by the sheer *range* of choices (what colors? which fabrics? what pieces of furniture?) that we become paralyzed.

Because our house was in such bad condition when we purchased it, we knew we would have to spend months renovating the inside and out. True, I could visualize the sun flooding into those spaces after we washed them in a bath of pure white paint,

Creating a beautiful home is a high artistic achievement; enjoying it is the art of living.

but what then? We decided to spend some time just camping out in the house, to let the spaces speak to us and allow us to know the rooms firsthand. (We discovered that camping out is one sure way of discovering what you want to do.) And slowly we learned that our house was utterly charming and wanted only to be loved, not completely made over. The rooms were ideal for comfort and pleasant conversations — and that was the spirit we set out to address.

Taking action galvanizes the spirit and unleashes blocked energy. Yet we all resist taking the first step, even though once we do, we immediately feel better — and more confident. My friend Kate says, "Action begets action." When you do one thing, you cut through that "stuck" feeling and build a momentum.

Most important, once you've examined your own lifestyle preferences, decisions about decorating will come naturally. Start by asking yourself questions: Do you like spare, spartan rooms, or do you prefer cozy clutter? Are you looking for a dramatic or a serene effect? What are some of your favorite pieces of furniture? Ask yourself *why* you like them — and never be afraid to surround yourself with things you have chosen because of their special meaning for *you*. And finally, try to analyze your specific, current needs, and consider ways in which your home may evolve to meet them without destroying the spirit of your place or your evolving aesthetic.

When something appears to be simple it is often deceptively difficult to achieve.

*T*EN SECRETS TO FINDING YOUR PERSONAL DECORATING STYLE

In my decorating business being a good listener has helped me translate the needs and fantasies of my clients into the right designs for their homes. One client repeatedly told me that she wanted her living room to be peaceful and serene, yet the colors she was drawn to were red, peach, and bright yellow — hardly meditative tones. When I asked her how she wanted to feel when she walked into the room, she said she wanted everything to flow gently together. "I don't like busy things," she said, waving her hands in the air. It suddenly became clear to me that it was *patterns* that made her nervous. By listening to her, I was able to give her the vital hues she loved and, by using solid colors, the feeling of calm she needed.

People invariably reveal themselves in conversation once you are alert and listen for signals. We can accomplish the same things by simply looking inside ourselves, by asking the right questions, and by paying attention to our answers. *Self-awareness inevitably leads to self-expression.* As you set about creating the living space that will suit you now and be adaptable throughout the years, as your needs and priorities grow and change with the times, the place to begin is to know who *you* are, and what your personal (or familiar) lifestyle *is.*

1. Your Personality Reveals Your Style

Get in touch with that spirit inside you. Who you are is a coming together of everything you've been exposed to all your life, how you've grown and changed, what you aspire to, and (most important) what you respond to emotionally. Style really comes down to what makes you feel good. I knew early on that I respond to light and to clear, fresh, bright colors. Look inside my clothes and linen closets, and you'll see a riot of color. We may believe that when it comes to choosing a wardrobe we're all impulse shoppers, but I don't agree. Do you want to decorate with patterns or predominantly with solids? With lively hues, pastels, or earth tones? One way to determine what you can live with is by looking at what you already *do*. Important clues to decoding your personality and style lurk right in your own closets. Open up those doors! It's all there. The colors you like to wear may very well be those that will make you feel comfortable in the rooms of your home. It's that simple.

My style is light and natural colors, refinement and elegance.

On a more fundamental level, you can identify your own decorating style by simply examining your personality, because who you are will connect all the various design details into a cohesive whole. Are you by nature reserved? If you are, you will probably feel more at home surrounded with subtle tones, and you'll probably choose classic period furnishings. The refined details and soft, muted colors of your surroundings will evoke an earlier time in history, and the art and accessories you choose are likely to be of above-average quality. Or if you are more outgoing and flamboyant, you will be drawn to spontaneous originality as a means of self-expression. You may be more likely to take risks and chances with your decorating, believing that there is something interesting to convey in anything, no matter how unconventional. For instance, you might prefer to substitute a natural maple cutting board for a graceful silver tray on which to display painted pottery rather than your grandmother's delicate china tea set, or opt to use an unfinished marble slab to show a piece of sculpture instead of a traditional stand.

Whoever you are, do not deny it. Celebrate it. Successful decorating reveals the atmosphere of the inner self. Unless your decorating style—the outer expression of who you are—is in harmony with your inner self, you won't feel the proper rhythm that is so essential in all aesthetic compositions. Remember, style emerges when you accept yourself. But as you analyze your personal decorating style, be encouraged to push that envelope a bit. For example, if you are extremely shy and have been hiding behind beige, perhaps you can make a conscious effort to be more daring and let your rooms reflect a more emboldened attitude. When I asked a client if beige was a favorite color because that is all I saw in her apartment, Deborah laughed. "It's true. I'm a contemplative person, and don't like to reveal a great deal about myself to others." However, when we looked at the swatch book of paint colors, she saw how the all-beige living room could

Art is not handicraft but rather the offspring of a touch of genius.
— Peter Megargee Brown

be transformed into a more expressive room by painting the trim white and the walls a pale, soft yellow without violating the integrity of her natural tastes and preferences. Often, our style selections let us know we need to make an effort to reach out beyond the safe and the bland.

2. Start with Where You Are *Now*

Starting is half-finished. Be aware that everything will evolve and change as you mature, and as your needs and circumstances change. Possibly you did buy your dream house and took on more than you could comfortably afford. You'll have to cut way back until you get on your feet again, or proceed slowly, budgeting carefully, and prioritizing your choices. One young couple saved up in order to paint what had been dull-colored rooms into fresh, cheerful, inviting ones. Others enjoy a few sparsely furnished rooms. The Japanese believe that "space to breathe" is psychologically important. You may have bought your house because you desperately needed more space, emotionally and physically. Enjoy pure space and slowly build from that. Paint a room a favorite color. How many of us have the luxury of a personally colored, empty room—a hope chest for our future? The important thing is not to feel compelled to do everything all at once, or be embarrassed if you can't. Time has a way of filling empty rooms—and inspiration often comes with time.

It's also important that our decisions at home are informed by where we are in our lives and in our relationship *with others*. Sometimes, what *we* want just isn't practical or right for us now. A home with small children *should* be set up differently than one with grown children. If you're divorced or remarried and stepchildren visit you often, you'll have to make appropriate arrangements for them. These are not so much questions of lifestyle as of life *passages*. The practical considerations, realistically addressed, will help you to manipulate your rooms to serve a particular situation.

Be faithful to your own taste because nothing you really like is ever out of style.
—Billy Baldwin

We all experience these life cycles; how and where we are in them inform the choices we make, room by room. The actual usefulness of a space is what counts. Explore new alternatives. If you have preschool children, perhaps you can turn the dining room into a play area, temporarily storing the table and chairs. The hours of fun your children will enjoy in this space seem more important than an occasional dinner party. Similarly, that blinding white upholstery you've envisioned for your living room should probably be deferred until your children are older, when your rooms can be freshened and become more refined; and your limited resources are probably better reserved for renovating the back of the house to make that large family room you can *all* enjoy now. Clients who married and inherited stepchildren turned their dining room into a bedroom for their two teenage daughters, knowing they could reclaim it when the girls graduated from college. By putting a table in the front hall, they created an eating area. You cannot pretend that a given situation doesn't exist. There are creative solutions to almost any circumstance. You must search for these.

Nothing should be stuck in concrete. When a child expresses a need for privacy, and is sharing a room with a sibling, you can give up a room temporarily. Remember, you're talking about a few years—and about people you love.

An honest home that rings true to the lives of the people who occupy it will always be disarmingly refreshing to visitors. But when that chapter is over, everything can be rethought. If the playroom off the kitchen you created for your boys is no longer used, because the boys are teenagers now and require private space for themselves and their friends, you can move the boys downstairs to a refinished basement and recapture the playroom for yourself—a studio, writing room, or garden room. To leave space the way it was when it once was alive and vital is a waste of opportunities for new life passages.

Almost everything is a memento from our travels.
—Rodalfo Machado, architect

3. Contour Your Environment to Suit Your Unique Needs

A spouse often comes home from work with one intention in mind. Bill wanted to make a drink for himself, go to the family room, and read with his six-year-old son. But the antique coffee table was all wrong—it was too small, too high, and too fragile to put his feet up on it comfortably. The butler's tray table was moved to the wall, where it holds current magazines and books. Bill now has a large, modern coffee table in front of the sofa, so he can put his feet up, he and his child can have a place for their drinks and snacks, and there is space to rest some additional books. If you enjoy putting your feet up when relaxing privately at home, plan to have a sturdy, low table.

A friend was under doctor's orders to stay in bed during the final months of a difficult pregnancy. Rather than being isolated in her upstairs bedroom, Kathy had her bed moved down to the living room where she could enjoy the activities of her family as well as have the warmth of the fireplace, views of the garden and yard, and two walls of bookcases for some of her favorite books and musical equipment to help pass the time. Living rooms (as I keep saying) are for living. Manipulate your spaces, and don't be afraid to break the rules.

This is exactly what a client did when she called to inquire if I could help turn the screened porch of their house into a sitting room/bedroom for her husband, who was recuperating from major surgery. John would shortly be coming home from the hospital, but his recovery would be more complete if he didn't have to negotiate stairs. Another one of my clients loves rising early to enjoy a leisurely breakfast in the kitchen in her bathrobe. "The dining room is too formal for breakfast," she said. So Grace had a loveseat and bay window installed in her breakfast nook, making for comfortable, relaxed mornings at the kitchen farm table where she can read the paper, consult her calendar, and

Ease at home has to do with attitude and value. Luxury and elegance can always be understated and relaxed.

enjoy a few moments' peace before she has to dress and leave for the office. Another friend, an avid urban gardener, turned her second bathroom into a potting shed by installing a hinged counter under the vanity. The secret is to utilize *all* your space so it functions as well as pleases you, depending on the time of day, your mood, and your needs.

Our Connecticut living room is made up of two separate spaces, joined by an arch with bookcases on either side, in both rooms. Under the arch of each space, we placed a round table. I've claimed this space to do my writing and my correspondence, and to nip into stacks of books piled high all around the table. Conveniently, this is an ideal spot to watch the sunset as well as to observe the activities around me. The fact that the space is all set up with a cup of pens, paper clips, flowers, a lamp, a candle, and lots of books gives me the feeling that a sacred place is waiting for me. Too few people really do useful work in their living rooms. A room that is all set up for company without the party is a dried-up room. It's far easier to tidy up a bit when you have friends over than to allow a room to go unused—and unenjoyed.

Rethink each room in your home. If you like, rename them so they are real to you. A client, concerned that her living room not feel stiff and too formal, calls it the library. Rich woods, books, flowers, paintings, and a favorite striped chintz make a warm, intimate, inviting, relaxing room. Books are read in this room, naps are taken here, and desk work is accomplished at the secretary.

If you have a son living at home who is heavily into sports, you might choose to turn a small downstairs bathroom into a stall shower so he doesn't have to share the bath with his sisters. When he goes off to college, you can reclaim this space, converting it into a sunny, cozy laundry room so you don't have to go down to the dark, dank basement to do the wash. A client did this, setting up the ironing board so that light spills down on

I like lots of air, order, personal objects and beautiful architecture.
—William Hodgins

her when she presses a blouse or pillow case. Remember, rooms are opportunities for real living to take place. Constantly run reality checks on your rooms so that you can enjoy them through the changing seasons of your life.

4. Create Your Own Reality

You can have a romantic country bedroom even if you live in a noisy, urban environment. Your feelings about life, the places you've traveled to, your favorite things, all give your home a personal signature. Inside, where you live, you are free to express yourself in unique ways, however fanciful. I take a real delight in having old white wicker in my New York bedroom because it reminds me of carefree summer afternoons, all year round. Let your dreams and fantasies about how you want a room to look and feel create their solution. Just because we live in a certain part of the country doesn't mean we should restrict our imagination from living inside our dream house. A client who moved to New York from Tokyo wanted to re-create peaceful surroundings that would remind her of where she lived in Japan. By building sliding walls covered in natural-colored silk bordered in black lacquer, Meg was able to slide the four-foot-wide panels back to reveal a picture or keep them closed to provide a calm, serene mood. Even at the windows, the translucent silk panels slide across the glass when necessary for privacy, allowing the light to come into the space.

Another client who lives on the eleventh floor of an urban apartment felt frustrated that she couldn't see trees or grass, or any signs of nature from her windows. We installed white wooden flower boxes *inside* her living room windows, supported on angle irons. By lining the boxes in a plastic plant container, Barbara is able to alternate a variety of seasonal flowering plants purchased inexpensively at the farmers' market. With the help of Miracle-Gro her indoor garden thrives year round. Because

Some rooms have the genius of poetry.

❖

we're used to seeing outdoor window boxes, when they're used indoors, they fool the eye into associating the flowering plants they contain with grass, trees, and a garden.

Similarly, in our New York apartment our family room has a bad view of another building. We hung white vinyl roller shades, which are always kept down. By installing tubular incandescent light strips on the four sides of the windows, and by hanging white shutters across the front, it appears as though the sun is always shining. This adaptable principle can be used in any room that has an ugly view. The windows can still be opened for air, but the illusion of light where there is none will remain. I've used this idea in children's rooms also. The light lifts everyone's spirit.

All of us have preferences for certain kinds of architecture and period regional styles that we would like to incorporate into our rooms. We can re-create them slavishly, or use the past and its established reference points to make fresh, original statements.

Friends of ours who live in an old brick house in South Carolina found themselves drawn equally to English and French country styles. So they opted for both (again flouting the rules), decorating the downstairs in the English manner, while the bedrooms upstairs are a bit fancier, more feminine, combining the styles of Louis XV and Louis XVI. The curtains upstairs are tied back in a poufy balloon style, while downstairs they are straight-hanging. And why not?

Feel free to create at least one room that is different from the others. For example, my upstairs writing room is as spare as the rest of my house is happily cluttered, consisting of a simple table and hardwood side chair. I call this room my "Zen room." The spareness gives my soul space to breathe (and I don't need anyone suggesting I get a computer!); and the room is definitely off-limits to everyone but me. But whether you limit your fantasy to just one room or bring it into the whole house, remember: No authentic period style should ever get in the way of creating your

Adornment is never anything except a reflection of the heart.
—Coco Chanel

own fantasy. The classic traditions are only guides to help you achieve your dreams. We are limited only by the poverty of our own imaginative leaps.

5. Do Your Homework

When you get excited about something, read all you can about it. The more you learn, the more you can appreciate what's around you and feel the interconnectedness of the elements. Not all of us studied the decorative arts at Harvard, but we can educate ourselves, analyze what we like, ask questions, take notes in a special "Home" notebook, and make better choices because we understand why we make them.

Whenever clients tell me they don't know what they want, I ask them to rip out pictures of what they like from magazines. I tell them to clear their heads of all agendas and preconceptions and just to be spontaneous. Magazines, in fact, can be extremely useful as a means of focusing our efforts. We not only see what's available to use in our own homes, we can also get ideas and inspiration from the variety of ways in which the details were put together by someone else.

This is exactly what Joanna did, the woman who fell in love with that surprising house on the hill. But after she and her family moved in, she was overcome by the range of decorating decisions she now confronted. What overall style did she like? She didn't know: She liked many types of rooms. What look was she after? Classical? But could classical still be dramatic? Could dramatic still be comfortable? Cozy clutter? But her rooms were small. Wouldn't too many pieces overwhelm them? Would too much clutter appear "precious," too little, spartan?

After months of poring over magazines and tearing out whatever appealed to her (without stopping to think why), her design folder began to bulge with pictures of conflicting window treatments and incompatible furniture combinations. Finally, certain

True art is in the doing of it.
— *Jean Renoir*

patterns and themes began to emerge. She found, to her surprise, that she wasn't a carpet person and that she had outgrown the country pine look she had loved when she lived in the city, when all she could do was escape to the country for quiet weekends. And then one day, she saw "it": a home designed by its owners to respect what they called the house's "unpretentious formality." Simplicity with understated elegance. It was the living room floors that stopped her cold—wide bands of alternating stained floorboards that gave the room the drama Joanna was seeking without overwhelming the rest. Suddenly, everything clicked for her, and she knew just where to begin. By making the floors her priority, she was able to move on and make appropriate decisions about wall and window treatments, fabrics, and upholstered pieces. Everything came together once she had committed herself to start with the floors.

Decorating is an intuitive process, but it is also a complex art form because of the myriad of elements and details that have to harmonize. Each of us—whether we feel we are innately creative or not—can benefit by taking advantage of opportunities to school ourselves. Whenever you are in the beautiful rooms of friends or acquaintances, and it is appropriate, ask to have a tour of the house and/or gardens. Inquire about the art, furniture, and landscaping. This is what decorators do; it's how we continue to learn and improve our craft. It's instructive to draw on other visions and insights, and to adapt and make them our own, in accordance with our finances and the limits of our own spaces.

So, go to the old, restored houses that are open to the public. Take guided tours, visit the decorator show houses, and take notes. Make it a regular habit to attend lectures to hear what interior and landscape designers, architects, and decorative arts scholars have to say. Slide presentations can illuminate a strategy, theory, or design principle. Seeing is believing—and understanding.

Illustrated books are also a good source for you, but they are

*Pay attention to
every detail.*

often too expensive to buy. On the other hand, publishers sometimes remainder these books making them available at a modest cost. When I was in art school, I was able to build up an art and design library by going regularly to bookstores and street fairs. Don't pass up a good book value that will help you train your eye. Your own reference library of the decorative arts will yield continuous inspiration and design solutions.

I advise my clients to keep all their notes about the home in an 8½ by 11-inch spiral notebook. Get one that has pouches for storing magazine pictures, fabric cuttings, estimates, and invoices, and with dividers for specific areas you are working on. Record product information, phone numbers, measurements, and supplier information. You can sketch details or room arrangements or attach paint samples. You will find your "Home" book an invaluable tool to help you accomplish your decorating goals.

Every bit of effort and every bit of information help. Seldom do we have a clear vision of what we want. The more we see, read, and study, the easier it is to define, and refine, our decorating goals.

6. Examine Your Own Life

Often the wellspring for creative breakthroughs is simply inside you, waiting for you to seize it and bring it to life. A client became frustrated when I walked around her house without taking notes. "Alexandra, are you going to remember all this?" she asked. I smiled. "No, not everything, but what's important, I'll remember. First I have to absorb the whole."

Think back and reflect on where you've been — examine your far past as well as your near past, the influences that shaped you and define you still. Look for the connections, the things that repeat themselves. They may be as primal as your earliest childhood memories (for me, it is the memory of happy afternoons playing in my mother's garden, which instilled in me the passion

We forget three fourths of ourselves to be like other people.
—Arthur Schopenhauer

for flowers and natural beauty that has become the signature of my professional design aesthetic); summers spent at the lake or in the mountains, or doing the things you love doing now. Your own history can give you suggestions about themes and subjects that will add individuality to your decorating.

Are there some activities you enjoyed at an earlier period of your life that you'd like to incorporate into your decorating? For instance, while I no longer play tennis because of a tricky back, I was a fairly accomplished player and I loved the game. A few photographs in the library of me on the court is a reference to this past that gives me a warm feeling of continuity. Peter, too, likes to have all his legal paraphernalia around him in his writing room — his gavels, scales, and law books, as well as photographs of some of the judges, lawyers, and colleagues he most admires. The point is that nothing in decorating should come out of the blue or in isolation. Everything is interconnected. Your past and its memorabilia, your long-ago and current interests, the sports you enjoy, the trips you have taken, your family and friends — all bring a richness to your decorating schemes. And sometimes they may actually define them.

This is exactly what happened with Wendy, who lives in suburban Chicago. When Wendy purchased her house, she had that same "stuck" feeling that so many of us have. Although she was living a thousand miles away from the small Pennsylvania town she was born in, whenever she closed her eyes and let her mind take over, she kept remembering her childhood days. Gentle memories of rolling hills and pasturelands; of farmers carrying their fresh produce to country markets; of home-made country jams and tart apple ciders; of country crafts like colorful quilted bedding and the tin miniatures her grandfather used to collect. Suddenly she understood that this same country spirit, which had shaped her, was the essence of what she wanted her home to capture.

They say you can't go home again, but Wendy did. Each time

Much of the character of everyman may be read in his house.
— John Ruskin

she returned to see her family, who still lived in the area, she would visit country artisans and craftspeople, local antique dealers and collectors; and after a while she began to put her home together, room by room, from the hand-made quilt hanging on her living-room wall, to the hand-hammered tin light fixture she commissioned for her dining room, to the superb painted antique armoire in her bedroom. Her house bears little affinity to the postmodern chic of her sophisticated neighbors and friends . . . but they have come to admire her house because it is uniquely *hers*. Wendy herself also understands that the decoration of her house is not only a tribute to the ways and traditions of her ancestors, but that it has made that heritage come alive for her children, who might otherwise grow up feeling disassociated and detached from it.

Individuality and personality cannot be manufactured, but I do believe we can dig inside of ourselves and tap into it. In Wendy's case, what arose out of the most mundane requirement of filling a house became a personal passion. Today, she is widely read and something of an expert on the folk art not just of her native Pennsylvania, but of many cultures and societies, and she has enhanced her home with examples from these other collections. And, incidentally, she recently fulfilled her vision by drawing on her love of the folk arts by commissioning (working with a student artist) a life-sized watercolor painting of her children, in the tradition of nineteenth-century American folk art portraiture. It is a remarkable (and not unaffordable) departure from the banal and overpriced efforts of child-portrait studios.

As Wendy found, the only meaningful decorating style is one that is original. You can't copy someone else's lifestyle and ever set it really right. Personal style is best achieved by following your intuition, and your heart.

Taste is an expression of your exposure.
— *Walter Hoving*

7. Trust Your Eye and Be Alert to Your Senses

I am often asked if good taste is something we can acquire. My answer to this is a resounding yes! Some people do have innate taste, but for most of us, good taste emerges once we have learned to trust our own eyes. If you are drawn to certain colors and objects, chances are that a compatibility of spirit will bind them together. Even if the things you cherish aren't of the same vintage and design, you can combine them successfully. Repetition of material, form, or scale provides harmony.

Taste—for food and drink, as well as things visual—is the key to self-awareness and expression. You absorb taste and refine it over your lifetime. Taste has to do with selection—and how you combine it with your personal style.

Your eye will guide you in your quest. Use daily life as your tutor. Look at the details, the shapes, forms, proportions, textures, and colors of everything around you. Look at patterns and the way things are arranged. Go to museums and feast your eye on the best: The more quality your eye sees, the more discerning it becomes.

There is much around us that is pretentious and ugly. A professor in design school taught his students that they would have to edit out roughly 90 percent of everything that is available in furniture, textiles, and colors and then choose carefully and judiciously from the remaining 10 percent. You, too, can gather what is meaningful from approximately 10 percent of everything you are exposed to and then use that selection as a well to draw from.

You be the judge. Be true to yourself and your taste will be genuine and speak to you viscerally. You will outgrow some of your current tastes in years to come. I went through some awful phases that today make me cringe to think about—fake Spanish Colonial, awkward wrought-iron objects, gaudy colors. But I

Seek freshness and lightness.

*Many people have
eyesight but real
seeing is rare.*

loved my first apartment! Learn to trust your instincts. Taste is acquired by trial and error, like an artist who builds a canvas with color to create form and light. Keep an open mind. Record your impressions honestly and you will grow in your level of appreciation and in nuance. When you weed out the negative 90 percent of what you see around you, the personally pleasurable 10 percent that remains will give you a clearer, more confident picture of who you are.

One way of arriving at this is by being alert to how our senses affect us. For instance, the sense of smell is a subtle but helpful stimulus that may help us to create moods for our rooms. This is because our olfactory sense sends messages to the area of the brain that deals with emotions and memories. Lemon scents refresh. Jasmine makes us drowsy. Peppermint stimulates. Lavender soothes. What do your favorite scents tell you about *you*?

Think, too, about the textures in your life. What kind of fabric do you want for your desk chair? You may want to select a soft fabric (a cotton chintz or a velvet) for a seat cover because you enjoy sitting at your desk in your nightgown, and most other fabrics are scratchy and might cause irritation. Throw pillows can be covered in more sensuous fabrics because we tend to play with pillows and hug them. When you touch something, become aware of where you intend to use it. The feel of a sisal rug to your sensitive bare feet could be a turn-off; the cool temperature of marble, a turn-on.

The important thing to remember as you begin to make choices is to feel things, to allow impressions to register, and then to *react*. Run your hands along the surface of a table and then feel underneath it. Feel your wall surfaces and countertops. When you try on clothes, don't you make sure that the fabric doesn't itch and that there are no uncomfortable seams or bulky labels to irritate you?

Our responses to the tactile, surface areas of the home should pass those same tests. The more pleasing and intimate they are, the more delighted and comfortable we feel.

As you contemplate your design decisions and try to establish priorities, simply list the five God-given senses:

sight

touch

taste

smell

sound

I have rated my own senses from one to five by listing them in order of importance and development. For me, sight is, not surprisingly, first. Next comes touch, which includes sensual pleasures and the feel of marble, cotton, porcelain, paper, a warm bath, soft bedclothes. Third, I list taste because I have a passion for good food, and so my kitchen and dining spaces have a special importance. I rate smell fourth because of the carefree childhood memories and associations the olfactory sense calls forth. My love of gardening and cooking is surely multiplied by the sweet aromas of flowers and food. To be able to smell spring, the sea, a hyacinth, a newborn baby, and freshly baked bread makes me happy and gives me hope. Sound is number five. I can be moved to tears by beautiful music, and I adore the timbre of laughter and loving conversation. But I definitely rate sound as the least personally significant of the five senses—and the decoration of my home reflects my sense priorities.

We are all sentient beings and each one of us feels a little differently about the five senses. I've asked friends and acquaintances how they rate theirs, and in every case, it is most revealing. Charles is an artist and a wine collector, and he lists sight first, taste second, touch third, sound fourth, smell last. His home is done in deep burgundies and golds, with dark-stained mahogany floors. My friend Elisabeth places sight first, then sound, smell, touch, and taste. Her Manhattan loft has glorious city

Composition is the art of arranging.
— Henri Matisse

views—and Thermopane double windows to shield herself from city noises. Bill is a musician. He places sound first, then taste, sight, touch, and smell. Not unexpectedly he put a lot of money into the walls—for his stereo and shelving for his music collection—and into a commercially designed kitchen/living area, which is perfect for the casual, drop-in entertaining he likes to host. Barbara puts touch first—lots of faux-painted wall surfaces—hearing second, smell third, taste fourth, and sight fifth. What about you?

Obviously, there is no good or bad score in this rating game, the purpose of which is simply to help us identify priorities and develop a personal sense of taste. Our senses help us enhance and appreciate the beauty in our surroundings. The more beauty we can experience at home, the more strength and pleasure we will derive from our precious home time. Indeed, even the details of everyday living offer us sensory opportunities. A drawer can be lined with a pretty piece of fabric or a favorite marbleized paper. Even a shelf can be lined or banded with a contrasting paint color or trimmed with a colorful grosgrain ribbon.

We are in the flow of home when we have our favorite books, a good reading light, and soft pillows to snuggle into; when we have sparkling colors, the fresh scent of flowers, natural light, and the freedom to be the authentic person we are. Add to this some solitude and some companionship, and we have effected the continuity of spirit and place that defines personal style.

8. Edit, Putter, and Eliminate

Control, edit and distill.
—Van Day Truex

❖

Style requires discipline. After you understand the range and consequences of your choices, you must begin to eliminate or edit out what you don't like or need or want. The best way to see your personal style emerge is to go through your rooms and admit that some things you liked in an earlier life no longer attract you. Whatever you don't want can probably be enjoyed by someone else because each of us is in a different place in our style journey.

"Creative puttering" is actually one of my favorite things to do at home. When I putter, I begin by straightening up—dusting, rearranging objects on a tabletop, putting things in order. To some extent, I move about on automatic pilot, letting instinct take over. I try to stay open to every delight, but if I see something that doesn't please me, I correct it or eliminate it entirely. I might replace a dried-flower basket with an arrangement of fresh flowers, because the season has changed and the winter arrangement now looks tired. I may rearrange a group of family pictures to update them, or rearrange the crockery in the cupboard. Puttering gives me instant satisfaction because the results are immediate—and it makes my rooms feel more spontaneous.

But puttering is more than just a useful ritual to edit out the accumulation and mass we've grown to tolerate. It helps us to become aware of what's still important to us, what continues to have meaning. This quiet, private act can therefore become an agent in helping us discover more about our feelings and our personal evolution. Like the prepartum "nesting" instinct, removing clutter prepares us mentally and our homes physically to make way for the new, and to improve our surroundings.

Puttering is also a useful way to bring the different aspects of your life into sharp focus—and to identify your needs. Just as the decision to preserve things underscores our affection for them, what we eliminate helps determine what must be replaced, or filled in, thus allowing us to establish goals and priorities. If your front hall table has become cluttered, straighten it up, toss out the old mail, and rearrange all the objects. While you are looking at the table with fresh eyes, you may decide it's time for a pick-me-up. You may plan to repaint it an entirely fresh color; you may decide it's no longer serving your needs, and it needs replacing.

Because the decoration of our interiors must always be a

Nothing is ever wasted if it makes a happy memory.

changing landscape, puttering helps keep us up-to-date with our attachment to the things in our home. By reevaluating our possessions we may be inspired to seize the opportunity for fresh starts. We must remain free to let go of the old and tired—whether this means restuffing and reupholstering a favorite reading chair, or giving an entire room or a corner of it a facelift—to make way for the new and exciting.

9. Simplicity, Appropriateness, and Beauty

For over twenty years I've discussed my formula for art and design, a triangle of Simplicity, Appropriateness, and Beauty. In *Daring to Be Yourself*, I showed readers how useful this principle can be in making personal style decisions—from home entertaining to choosing a wardrobe; from making plans to deciding how to spend your leisure time; but nowhere is this trinity of goals more meaningful than in helping you bring that same personal style sense into all your decorating decisions. For as Li Liweng writes in *Art of Living*, "A house and the people living in it must harmonize as in a picture.... cherish the virtue of simplicity. For the important thing in a living house is not splendor, but refinement, not elaborate decorativeness, but novelty and elegance."

Rooms should look effortless and have an ease about them that soothes.

SIMPLICITY

You will never slip into pretentiousness or artificiality when you build your rooms on a solid foundation of simplicity. But most of us have a tendency to overdo, to reach for the most complicated (and usually costly) solution. Instead, try to keep in mind that less is more. When it comes to your rooms, think of them as intimate spaces where *you* want to feel comfortable, alone. Immediately you'll lose your fear of what others will think, or your impulse to overanalyze a decision—and to throw money at it. Elegance is more often achieved by what you leave out.

For instance, if you want light and to create a feeling of spaciousness, you might choose to paint the walls a fresh white. Before you decide on a ceiling fixture, consider closing up the outlet and lighting the room with decorative table lamps. Sconces: Do you want them? Are they necessary? Ask yourself: What is the simplest solution? And what can you do without.

Applied ornamentation, like a gooey, too sweet frosting on a cake, can come across as unctuous rather than attractive, charming, or in character. The more sophisticated your eye becomes, the more assured your personal style will be, the more easily you will reach for the most *authentic* decorating solution. Simplicity is no more than a fresh glint of sunshine in a room. Clean windows. Simple enough. Shiny waxed wood floors. Fresh flowers. Books. A writing desk. A beautiful painting. Some comfortable furniture. When we try to be too ambitious in the decoration of our rooms, we get off the track. Remember, decorating is really simple. Professionals get paid to make it complicated, but it doesn't have to be.

My style is a constant search for simplicity, elegance, and quality.
—Karl Springer

APPROPRIATENESS

I don't think I fully understood the meaning of appropriateness until I fell in love with our tiny cottage, with its peculiarly shaped spaces, curves, angles, and juts. We might have modernized the kitchen and the baths; we could have added bay windows and central air conditioning, but we decided to leave the house alone because, ultimately, the appropriate thing was to do nothing to change the structure. We retained the personality of an old cottage.

Ask yourself what is appropriate for your house, for you and your family, for your budget, and for the limits of your room dimensions. Limitations are *liberating*, and their solutions self-directing. Each room will then speak to you from a point of view that is naturally yours. *You* have to feel comfortable in the atmosphere you create. Your rooms have to work not only for you but for the unique habits, customs, and patterns of your family. A family who creates rigidly formal rooms, while also raising young children in them, sends out signals that pretty things or delicate fabrics are more important than small, growing people. So, the more appropriate your room choices are, the more happy and complete will be the life lived out in them—and they will sing out with an unshakable integrity.

Appropriateness, I want to emphasize, is not about money. Some people have a great deal of it, and can afford to spend whatever it takes on whatever strikes their fancy. Still, in my experience, the clients who tend most often toward excess can overwhelm a room's soul. Calculated sophistication, displays of conspicuous consumption, and rooms that are props—inanimate and impersonal—do not beckon to others and don't necessarily make you feel good, either. An appropriate room in a home should tell of the character, interests, and spirit of the people who live in it. Appropriateness is about authenticity. Most people loathe pretension. But when we decorate, we often put on masks and create aliases in the form of decorations that are fake, stale, monotonous, and banal. Artificiality is a hoax, no matter how well executed. So the secret to appropriateness is always to be yourself.

It takes time and patience to find your personal, original, and unique style. But once you are able to say, "That's not me. That's not right. That won't fit in. I can't afford it. I don't like it," then you will be much closer to defining and executing your very own decorating style.

*I deeply believe that a beautiful decor can have a beneficial influence on our lives.
— Albert Hadley*

BEAUTY

Once our personal style is deeply anchored in simplicity and appropriateness, then our rooms will reveal their own inward beauty. Beauty in a room requires a point of view, just as it does in a garden. I always think of rooms as gardens because they are similar in many ways. In order to work toward rooms that are in full bloom, you have to plant, tend, and nurture your space carefully. Gardeners know that they can't kill every weed or catch every falling leaf. So, too, our rooms can be perfectly beautiful without being immaculate or sterile. Gardeners aren't afraid to get dirty. I've even seen some of my gardening friends open a screen door, get a cool drink, and flop down in their gardening clothes on a club chair. That, after all, is the essence of beauty — to be able to relax spontaneously in your rooms. Being part of the creation of beauty, as well as appreciating that beauty at home every day, brings balance to your life.

Blend this trinity of simplicity, appropriateness, and beauty into your home as a natural extension of your personality. List on a sheet of paper all the things, tangible and intangible, that are beautiful to you. These are the physical, emotional, and spiritual elements that will inform your personal style and allow you to create a home that becomes a sacred place.

10. Treasure New Beginnings

Even if your house or apartment is already furnished, as you think about these secrets to finding your personal decorating style, you may experience your surroundings with a raised awareness. As I have said elsewhere, rooms are not still lifes; and the best of them, like life itself, continue to grow and change as we do. You will always be working and reworking, adding, adapting, rearranging, until a room is reborn. You don't have to do an entire makeover in order to bring some new creative energy and vitality into your living spaces. Little touches as you go along will bring you great satisfactions. A writer friend once told me, "You can't write Chapter two until you've lived and written Chapter one." I like this image of living our lives in chapters. It reminds us that change as well as continuity is natural to our lives.

There must be fitness, appropriateness, proportion, simplicity, harmony, and durability.
—Ella Church Rodman

Embrace all opportunities to upgrade your rooms as you go along, and don't be afraid to recognize that you want to, and can, make things better. Throughout your life, as family dynamics change, your rooms can, too. A new beginning could be when a child goes off to college or when you invest in a new home. Perhaps you're planning an addition, a renovation, or you're moving out of your neighborhood. My mentor, Mrs. Brown, warned us that one change can cause us to rethink everything and spark a chain reaction of decision-making. Whether it's repainting or redecorating, everything you do to your home will improve it, fine-tune it, and bring you into closer harmony with the person you are *now*. Rearranging objects, moving furniture around, hanging a new painting, replacing a piece of furniture, having a party, moving out, upgrading your furnishings, packing, unpacking, putting things up, making space for new beginnings are all part of the *empowering* process of life. You will feel exhilaration and joy in continuing to dream—and in the replenishment that is the essence and satisfaction of making your dreams real.

Minor changes can always be made later, but the point of view is there.
—Billy Baldwin

Chapter 4

THE ESSENTIAL
ELEMENTS OF
HOME DESIGN

Decorating today is a mirror shining and reflecting your light. When we decorate our homes, we express ourselves in a specific time. But just as two individuals can't have the same personality, neither can two real rooms. My mother, also a decorator, and I have very different tastes. Her style reflected her personality, her life's environmental influences as well as the fashions and social customs specific to her time. There's no question we've come a long way. If you reread old issues of *House & Garden* (*HG*) and *House Beautiful* from the 1950s, you'll laugh at the changes time has wrought in our attitudes and aesthetic sense. This is perhaps my best argument for having your rooms grow and change as you do. As we hone our taste and learn how to express ourselves, the mirror of decorating will reflect these changes naturally. But no matter what, our goal is always to have our rooms keep in touch with us.

When I began my career as a professional decorator in 1961, the mirror reflected something very different: a striving for perfection. Nothing less was acceptable. Clients paid us dearly to have everything properly scaled, correctly proportioned, immaculately right, down to the last detail. When the decorator placed an object on a table, there it had to remain, year in and year out.

An interior designer can never design your life.

53

Good taste and bad taste, adventurous and timid taste, cannot be explained by wealth or education, by breeding or background.
—Russell Lynes

The decorator knew best. Clients were to be careful not to disrupt the perfect placement, and were discouraged from showing anything personal, unless it was of the finest quality, for fear it would look out of place or, worse yet, sentimental.

But as department stores and shelter magazines began to display attractive rooms that people could assemble themselves, decorating became more eclectic. Department store decorators with flair put rooms together that borrowed from many different periods and international styles, that celebrated these differences and whetted people's appetite to add touches they responded to instinctively. By being exposed to these displays, all of us were liberated to loosen up and have fun collecting and gathering the things we liked. And magazines offered many specific strategies to encourage people to express their own personalities in decorating.

I have long felt that the more involved you are with your rooms, the more they will reflect the way you currently feel and see things. There is nothing more exciting than to change the way you look at things to envision something different from what already exists, and to slowly, gently, give your rooms your imprint. When you enjoy touching and rearranging things, trying a different furniture placement, moving a lamp to another table, *you* move in and become your own decorator.

The historical evolution of our houses from a series of perfect rooms to a temple of our autobiographies has also enabled us to rethink our attitude about the way we put together our homes. It's no longer important that they reflect that we "live well" (i.e., as evidence of our social status and wealth), but rather we want them to reflect good *living*. For who among us live perfect lives? Who would then choose to have perfect rooms? The satisfactions come from expressing ourselves. As I wrote earlier, whenever you try to achieve perfection in anything, you fall short of your unrealistic expectations. If I sell a lacquered table to a client, I explain that the chances of it getting to their living room un-

scratched are next to impossible. And the first time that the table is put to use, I guarantee that scratches will appear. What's finally important is that that table is no more than a well-loved symbol of the good living that takes place on and around it. Once you understand that, it's liberating. You have to learn to let go.

ZEN AND THE ART OF MISTAKE

Now that you've begun to define your personal decorating style, you will still have to make many hard design decisions; but you can begin to make them from a liberated perspective rather than feeling slavish about some unobtainable ideal. Liberation from bondage is freeing. If you choose to create a charming atmosphere for yourself, your family, and friends, this opens you up and allows you to make mistakes.

Decorating shouldn't be so studied or serious in the country. People should let accidents happen.
—Gary Hager, decorator

Who doesn't make mistakes? I've made so many, you'd be surprised. I have a friend who told me recently that "life is filled with brilliance, mystery, and mistake." Claire's motto applies to our decorating schemes, too. The reason I don't get overwhelmed by the mistakes I've made is because at least I've tried. There are a lot of people who never goof up, but they never take chances, either. Safe decorating is boring. And the last place in the world that should be boring is our home. If it is, we have only ourselves to blame.

A lesson I learned many years ago from a wise, successful client concerned what I've come to call the Zen of mistakes. I received a phone call at the office asking for an appointment. Later, in her living room, we enjoyed polite conversation over coffee until Pat told me that she'd made a decorating mistake. She didn't like the hunter green in the library. She'd lived with it for a month, but found it wasn't the right color for her. I was twenty-six years old, listening to a client reject the color scheme of a freshly finished decorated room. I was devastated. After all, *I* was the decorator. How could I face going back to my office? I'd been disgraced. I felt guilty. Tears welled up in my eyes as I tried to apologize. Pat comforted me with a hug. "Sandie, you have done nothing wrong. This is a beautiful library, but it is not right for me. I made a mistake, you didn't."

In the years since, I've discovered over and over how something can be right for one person and all wrong for someone else. And so I've tried to look at mistakes differently—to understand them individually. A mistake is something that is off-target for you. On the positive side, when we make mistakes—and we always do—we learn a great deal about ourselves in the process. Pat taught me an important lesson. She reminded me of the thousands of aesthetic choices she made that turned out to please her. "Perfection isn't my goal. I just want to feel pleased in my apartment. If I make a mistake, I can always correct it."

Most people who make a mistake try to pass the blame onto someone else. But whenever we try to do this, we never learn anything. When Alexandra and Brooke were born, I was living in a small, rent-controlled apartment. You entered into a long, narrow hall, which was ugly and depressing. I painted the walls dark brown, then sponged them and applied a coat of shiny clear lacquer to make them smile. The fashion craze at the time (the 1960s) was leopard carpeting. Because the hall was so painfully narrow, it needed wall-to-wall carpeting, and I fell for this jungle look.

The hall was also dark and richly textured, but I chose to light it with beaded-crystal light fixtures. Well, I can't tell you how ridiculous the hall looked. The sight of my adorable babies playing in this dark pseudoatmosphere was hopelessly incongruous. Fortunately, we were also bursting out of space and were able to move to a new apartment, where I had all the rooms painted bright white. The point is that I had been inspired to paint the walls a dark brown because I was trying to achieve a

What we have learned to do, we learn by doing.
—Aristotle

look made popular by the American interior designer Billy Baldwin, who lived in a tiny, very chic, all-brown apartment. But what a mistake to use this color in a cramped urban space with small children underfoot!

I tried so hard to have an attractive apartment that I lost sight of the fact that my daughters had no play area. The living room was done in pale yellow damask, better suited to a large house lived in by people no longer raising small, vigorous children. Whenever we are unrealistic about our limits, we make mistakes.

We can also mess up when we fail to accept the limits of our own spaces, as I did (I blush to say) in our Stonington house. We were in Copenhagen visiting friends and found at an antiques fair a painted Swedish cupboard that we thought would be ideal for the upstairs sitting room. It was the perfect piece, we anticipated, to hide the television and VCR when not in use, out of sight behind the hand-painted doors. When the truckers arrived, I showed one of them up the stairs through the tiny, narrow space that led to the sitting room. Returning down the staircase with me, he took off his baseball cap and scratched his head, and told me the grave news. "Mrs. Stoddard, this piece of furniture might have come from Copenhagen, but it isn't going any further than your living room. There is no way it can make the turns to get through those small openings that lead to the sitting room."

I was dumbfounded as I watched the rustic country cabinet planned for the family sitting room being deposited at the north end of our living room—where it contentedly resides today. Personal experience, painfully arrived at, has taught me to look at the Zen of mistakes with a bit more understanding. This wasn't just a question of taste or convenience—the piece was physically unable to go in the room where I'd intended it. Imagine if I'd bought that antique cupboard for a client; I wonder how pleased the person would have been!

Home is a day-to-day process which accommodates growth, change, and renewal.

Mistakes aren't all bad. The high piece looks as if it has always been in our living room. What we learned from this experience is that measurements alone aren't always reliable when considering placing a specific piece of furniture in a specific spot. It's easy to focus on whether or not something is an ideal size for a room, but not if you become blind to the practicalities of getting it there.

When Peter and I decided to turn a spare room into my writing room, we considered what sort of desk would look most attractive for the space, as well as be a comfortable size for me to work at. We wanted a humble farm table, which seemed to be a distant dream. Everything we saw was too fancy. One morning, as we were doing errands in our village, we stopped to look at a table in the window of an antique shop where we'd purchased other pieces for the house. The table was all right, but it wasn't what I had set my sights on. It was too orange in tone, and I didn't like its heavy, bulbous turned legs.

Then I weakened. The table wasn't perfect, but nothing is. I wanted something that came from a farm in the south of France, but here I was, in southeastern Connecticut, and I wanted to settle into my writing room. I rationalized that this table would be okay. After all, once I sat down to work, I wouldn't be aware of table legs. The surface would be covered with papers. Perhaps I could tone down the orange wood with a brown stain. The dealer offered to bring it over for me to try out. With little to lose, I accepted Michael's offer.

The next two hours were awkward and damaging as we tried to fit the table through our narrow upstairs doorways. It didn't. We reasoned that surely the back staircase would be more accommodating. Wrong. We removed more paint, dented more moldings. We removed doors from their hinges, bruised our knuckles, and finally gave up. There was no way this table could get to where it had to in order to be useful. I was defeated, but also spared. Had the table miraculously squeezed through im-

Be as genuine as you can so that your possessions will move with you wherever your life brings you.

possible dimensions, I would have been stuck with something I really didn't love. As the dealer walked the table back down the street, holding it upside down over his head, I sighed, listening to the silent voice that was telling me that I should be patient until the right thing came along.

I had also learned that dark, light-absorbing colors aren't right for the rooms where we spend daytime hours. When Peter and I got married, I moved into his apartment with Alexandra, who was six, and Brooke, who was four. Apparently, history repeats itself. I did it again. The kitchen in Peter's apartment was so awful I immediately suggested that we paint the plywood cabinets chocolate brown—the same color I had learned once wasn't right for me! But every situation is different, or so I told myself, and I was determined to have it. But as elegant and stylish as the brown cabinets were (so much so that the room was actually featured in a magazine as kitchen-of-the-month) I had to admit that the brown color was too rich and closed the room in. After years of living with this mistake, I finally changed the color to pale blue. Three strikes and you're out doesn't apply to decorating—and it didn't for me, either. While I was at it, I also lightened up the rich, Japanese lacquer-red of the library. We ended up painting it white after the girls requested a place to play with friends during the day. The lesson to learn from decorating is that you don't have to live with your mistakes. You can correct them.

Many people worry about expressing their personalities through their taste.
—Russell Lynes

My friends and clients continuously reinforce my attitude that it is often better to bite the bullet, cut your losses, and move on. This might seem easier said than done, especially when your good (and diminishing) money is involved. When a client bought an avocado refrigerator on sale at Macy's, she thought she would save money. The lure of the sale had excited Jane. The reality was that she loathed the color. Fortunately, she didn't go on decorating around this mistake, which happens more often than most people realize. She ended up having the refrigerator sprayed white—a reasonable solution to a potentially big problem.

A young wife and mother of two small children in North Carolina selected a fabric for the family's small pine-paneled study. Because the room was dark, Sarah thought she'd brighten it up with a white background linen print. When she went looking for fabrics with a friend, she found a large-scaled wild pattern she loved; it reminded her of her parents' sitting room in Santa Barbara. But in this diminutive study, the pattern looked all wrong. There was no mistake here; this was a clear disaster, understood by Sarah instantly. Fortunately, she had had the vision first to buy a yard of fabric in order to try it out, as often a small fabric swatch can be deceptive. This judgment call ensured damage control, and taught her an important lesson that we can all share.

Even when people hire talented decorators, there are no guarantees that what clients expect and how they will feel about things later will be the same.

A client ordered two expensive 8-foot-long brown Italian leather sofas. Even though she understood that the shade of leather can vary slightly from the sample, Laura was unpleasantly surprised when the furniture arrived. The color actually repulsed her; it reminded her of what I will delicately describe as "pooper-scooper" material. But she had ordered these sofas in a specific shade of tan leather, and now she was stuck. After the initial shock had passed, she gathered herself, and some additional money, together and had them slipcovered.

Even the most cautious can make surprise mistakes. A sweet client's husband retired at the same time we were redoing their living room. Mrs. Bell wanted her husband to be able to enjoy the room, so she suggested we use a practical, synthetic texture for his reading chair. The particular fabric we selected would never wear out: It was so fake, you couldn't burn it up. The problem was not evident right away, but the chair became grimy after a few months. It seemed to attract newspaper ink.

Perfection builds.
—Eleanor McMillen
Brown

Similarly, another woman wanted to protect furniture she inherited from her parents from wear and tear. She arranged to have a ¼-inch glass top cut for her dining room table. This would allow her not to worry about overwatering a basket centerpiece of African violets, as well as about the inevitable rings that result from sweating glasses. What a mistake! Andrea ended up with bleached, cracked, and dried wood (from sunlight reflecting on the glass top and heating the old wood). The good intention to protect heirloom furniture turned into a mistake that cost her money. She had to throw away the glass top and completely refinish the antique surface. Wax, polish, lots of good living, some coasters for drinks, and some dishes under flower baskets work wonders.

Mistakes happen. Some are obvious immediately. Others appear in time. Some mistakes occur out of innocence. A friend told me about the time she had ordered some expensive silk draperies for her living room—only to find, when the installer got on a ladder to hang the first curtain panel, that the material she believed she was getting was actually the back side of the swatch she had fallen in love with!

It is only what taste leads to that makes any difference in our lives.
—Russell Lynes

Whatever you do, take pride in doing your own decorating, and don't be too hard on yourself (or on your decorator, if you use one). What we should remember is that we're all human. We'll make mistakes. Anyone who hasn't made some real doozies is someone I wouldn't want to share a canoe with because I'd fear for their courage. Who likes to mess up? Who likes to admit the mistake? After all, we're all only trying to paddle upstream. We try, and we may err, but accepting that we're far from perfect ultimately brings us insight and understanding about ourselves.

I find that whenever I get off my path and try to be sophisticated or fancy, I mess up. I'm most useful to myself and others when I stick close to the bones of everyday life, and I would urge you to do the same. What we experience at home on a typical day is the best way to understand what real life is like.

Mistakes come in all shapes and sizes and surprises, but when we are honestly ourselves, the mistakes will be ones we will be more willing to admit and accept. Perfect people don't make mistakes, but you and I do—often. It's okay.

BUILDING BLOCKS—
THE ABC's OF SUCCESSFUL
ROOM DESIGN

A room is like the human body. It is alive, and needs to be well nourished and clothed. Some rooms are well proportioned, some have flaws, and others have beauty marks. Our rooms, like our bodies, grow and change over time, aging and maturing with us to accommodate our interests and new needs.

Rooms can grow and change as you want them to once you understand certain fundamental elements. You'll see that the way you choose to dress a room provides lots of latitude. When a room is young, it starts out with a basic wardrobe. As you and the room grow together, the room is clothed with color, texture, and the accessories that you love. Our toys change, but we all love to play with favorite things. Think of the different occasions where you celebrate the most important moments in your life. Make each room in your home come alive to reflect this spirit of ceremony.

Before moving toward complexity in the decision-making process of dressing a room, look at every room as having exactly the same elements. All rooms have walls, ceilings, floors, and windows. Fundamentally, we put furniture in our rooms. We light rooms artificially; we cover some furniture and some windows with fabric. We make color choices. We accessorize them with charming, personal, and well-loved objects. And all rooms, without exception, require maintenance. Ultimately, these are the building blocks of all rooms.

Taste in itself is nothing. It is only what taste lends itself to that makes any difference in our lives.
— Russell Lynes

Throughout this book, consider closely how these basic elements interact, and think about how they apply to your own home creations. Because certain rooms are allergic to a particular kind of treatment, each one will have to speak to you personally. It is essential that you look at the naked room first. Just as our bodies have some imperfections, few of us live in perfect rooms. We have to help out here and there to make the proportions more pleasing, bring in more light (both natural and artificial), and we have to play up the good points and play down the awkwardness. A little makeup or exercise always makes us look or feel better.

Rooms need to be understood uniquely. Where a room is situated, how the light patterns fall during the course of the day, how the light affects where you sit, the size of the room in relation to your size, the height of the ceiling in relation to room dimension and proportion—all of these are key. But equally important is to know how to mold, shape, manipulate, decorate, and color the rooms with your point of view. You have to look at the following ten room elements; focus on your present life, your needs, your actual space, and your aesthetic preferences:

Create a home with no waste spaces.

 walls

 ceilings

 floors

 windows

 furniture

 lighting

 fabric

⊞ color

⊞ accessories

⊞ maintenance

Photocopy a list of these essential elements for each of your rooms, to have handy to fill in your ideas. You'll see immediately that many of these room elements are interconnected, that they relate one to the other. Each element performs a different function, but all are connected and must work together.

When you think about the ten basic room elements, you may discover that you will want to repeat many of the same solutions, room by room. One decision links up to the next. Once you decide on the flooring in one room, the problems of adjoining floors are solved. Just as you can't wear too many different patterns without their clashing, the same applies to rooms. Too much of anything makes our eyes sore. If you choose to highlight your living room walls, you may decide to play down your floor treatment.

If you collect art, you automatically know that you have to keep your walls free of busy wallpaper. However, if you don't own any art, you may decide to have a high armoire as the room's visual focal point. One choice dictates other choices. By examining each element separately, you can see how to combine them, and decisions will then easily fall into place. If you choose light walls and ceiling, then perhaps you'll want a richer tone on your floor for contrast.

Study each element, evaluating its condition and charm. If you can't live with cracked, rough plaster walls, then you have to spackle and smooth them out with sandpaper before you paint. If your floor is covered, peel back a corner to see what's underneath. The floor may be of a beautiful hardwood that requires only patching, sanding, and a protective seal or perhaps a stain

We like the coexistence of different things in a room.
—Rodalfo Machado, architect

and some paste wax to bring it back to rich life. If the windows are small, you know you can't hide them behind heavy curtains. They'll look larger with white paint on all the trim. This decision alone solves the question of trim for the rest of the room.

What you do on one wall should be repeated on the other three. This concept is quite basic. Men's trouser legs that are made up of different colors front, back, left, and right, look silly like the clown's costume they usually are. But you *can* be more playful with the four walls of a child's room, where levity, not sophistication, is the name of the game.

When you try to interconnect the elements, you will see that solving one problem in a room automatically suggests a solution to another space. If you decide to bleach your own bedroom floor, for example, perhaps you could also bleach *all* the bedroom floors. If you select hardware for the front door, consider using the same door hardware throughout the house. If you like the Swedish enamel white paint you used in your living room for the woodwork — cornice molding, baseboard, chair rail, door trims, and window trims — think about using the exact same paint for all the woodwork in the house. If you do, you'll be grateful when you go around touching up chips and cracks with one paint can. Repeating elements simplifies maintenance.

When you find the upholstered chair that is properly scaled for your body, get other ones like it. A sofa and loveseat can be of the same design, scaled up or down, depending on length. You may choose a fabric and cover all your upholstery with it. Co-ordinating fabrics can be selected for chair cushions, pillows, a draped table cover, or a bench. Often, if you select a chintz fabric for your upholstered furniture, you will want to put the same chintz at the window. If, on the other hand, you choose solid, neutral textures, try a contrasting fabric at the windows, perhaps a wide-striped material, in order to pep things up.

People always ask me where to begin in a room — that is, which of the ten elements is most important to resolve first. Be-

To develop in taste, quality, and personality one is obliged to respect the past, accept the present, and look with enthusiasm toward the future.
—Eleanor McMillen Brown

cause each person sees his/her own rooms differently, I suggest that you begin with where you are and with what you have. If you have a favorite piece of furniture, find a place for it and work out the rest of the floor plan around it. If you have great wood floors, settle on their color so you can have the walls and ceiling complement them.

As you prepare to dress your rooms, imagine a naked body before it's covered up with colorful fabrics and accessories. Oftentimes, we can make the body look so great that we don't want to shroud it. There's something healthy and beautiful about a pure, empty room before it gets dressed. When you get the bones right, refining the bumps and bulges, smoothing out the skin of the walls with a fresh coat of paint, your rooms sparkle in their simplicity. And you'll usually be moved to add to the room's wardrobe more cautiously. For instance, when choosing a window treatment, you may hang inexpensive woven matchstick blinds for a more restrained solution to the question of privacy. Similarly, you can make a bulky air conditioner and ugly radiator disappear by painting them in a color that blends in with the rest of the room.

As I have already suggested, eliminate everything from your decorating vocabulary that you don't like. If you prefer solids to patterns, don't weaken now and try to get used to some fabric design you're not comfortable with. As you mature and experience more of life, your taste will change, but your rooms should never incorporate anything that you don't respond to emotionally.

Perhaps our deepest and most visceral responses concern color. My quest for freshness causes me to edit out colors that aren't pure pigment tinted with white but not toned down with gray, black, or gold. I love pastels and primary colors like clear red-pink fuchsia and pale peach, clear, clean yellows, greens of all clear, fresh shades, cool blues (like periwinkle), and all shades of purple, from deep indigo to pale lilac. I like rooms to have

Education, sensibility, and morality . . . these seem to me to be the components of taste.
— Russell Lynes,
The Tastemakers

approximately 75 percent white or a pale tint in them and 25 percent color; and I am especially drawn to white or yellow backgrounds for fabrics. But whatever colors draw you personally, create a color box in which to put scraps of color you like. This will help you build your own color palette so you can incorporate the tints and hues you love in your surroundings.

If colors have special meaning for us, so do objects. We accumulate accessories over a lifetime. They evolve naturally as our curiosity and interests deepen. These finishing touches to a room are like the buttons on a blazer or a favorite pin or bracelet, but a room cannot wear its entire accessory wardrobe at once, any more than you can pack all your clothes into one suitcase when you go on a holiday. Buy the accessories that you like as you go along and group them in categories according to similar scale, subject, category, material, color, and spirit. Accessorize judiciously, eliminating the dust collectors, the breakable, and the unnecessary. By carefully accessorizing your rooms with what you love, you create a mood and theme, variety and individuality for each space.

My professional decorating experiences have made me quite opinionated about how specifically to apply the ten room elements. Nonetheless, my design preferences can and *should* be different from yours. There is no reason not to take a different path, so long as it is informed by your unique point of view. As you begin to think about applying the ten design and structural elements that shape your rooms, remember that there is a wide variety of choice within each element. Choose the particular style of floor, window, lighting, etc., that works best for you, for each of your rooms, but keep in mind the functional and aesthetic aspects of each choice. Is it practical, economical, and purposeful? And is it simple, appropriate, and beautiful?

Every room needs a touch of yellow.
—Eleanor McMillen Brown

$\mathcal{P}$UTTING IT ALL TOGETHER: THE TEN COMMANDMENTS OF FABULOUS DECORATING

To help you transform your rooms into real spaces that speak of and for you, I have chosen ten general guidelines to consider as you make your decorating decisions. All these principles have a common denominator: They suggest solutions to typical missteps we all make along the way to achieving quality results.

1. Start Out with a Master Plan

Good rooms evolve. They grow, change, and become more refined and charming over time. When you plan your ideal room, and determine how you want it to look and feel, you can build toward that goal in a continuous process. Sketch out a floor plan so you know where you want the furniture to be placed. Don't design scared! Think of decorating as an *opportunity* to express your fantasies in color, form, scale, and lighting. Have the courage to create something original that uniquely pleases you, solves your practical needs and requirements, but that also reveals *your* taste and sense of style. Plan everything according to what would be best for each room. Have a long-range beautiful vision for each room that you can implement over time. For instance, you may replace a piece of furniture you already own but that you don't want now. Good work can't be rushed. Take your time. Think and plan ahead. Be bold.

It never occurred to me until I had this house to take a vacation and stay home.
—*Bill Robinson, decorator*

❖

2. Arrange Each Room with a Point of View and a Focal Point

No matter how beautiful your furnishings are, if you haven't decided on the style and resonance of the room, it will appear confused and awkward. Create a mood for each room. Decide whether you want rustic country, a Shaker simplicity, a French provincial character, or a sleek contemporary look. What gives a room its individual character is to focus on a feeling you can relate to. Establishing a room's theme will guide you into making the right selections and bring the disparate together into a whole. If you want to create a warm, friendly country atmosphere, avoid glass and lucite. Select warm wood and textured materials. On the other hand, if your taste runs toward modern design, have fewer elements but repeat them. For example, all the upholstered pieces can be of the same proportion as well as covered in the same fabric.

A room also needs a focal point—a main attraction. You should be able to walk into any room and be drawn to something powerful and beautiful. If you have a fireplace, the mantel should be handsome. Center a high piece of furniture prominently on a wall to draw the eye to it. A focal point can be anything from a great painting or a quilt on the wall to a piece of sculpture or a striking piece of furniture. Whatever you select—whether it be a four-poster bed or a fantastic secretary—let it be the exclamation mark in your room.

3. Don't Forget the Importance of Comfort and Convenience

We all want our rooms to look nice, but too often we neglect the obvious. If a room doesn't have comfortable furniture, if there isn't a reading light next to a chair or a place to put a drink and a book, a room won't feel right. Billy Baldwin, the legendary interior decorator, believed comfort was the ultimate success of a room. Install swivel mechanisms under your upholstered chairs. Create cozy seating areas where two people can sit together and enjoy an enriching conversation. If a room works for two people, it can be expanded to be comfortable for groups. Furniture must

Comfort and well-being can't be bought.

be flexible to be moved around whenever possible to accommodate different functional requirements.

4. Don't Ignore the Importance of Scale

The proportions of a room require specific scaled furnishings. If the ceilings are high, and you don't have a painting large enough to fill the space, it is better to hang a group of several smaller pictures on a wall above a table to create a harmonious arrangement. There should be a consistency of scale in your furniture. You can't place a tiny occasional chair adjacent to a ninety-inch sofa. One choice dictates the next. Always consider the human scale when deciding how large or small something should be. People must look and feel comfortable psychologically as well as physically. A man shouldn't feel that if he sits down in a fragile chair designed for a petite woman he'll break the legs off—or go through the caned seat.

I believe in plenty of optimism and white paint.
—Elsie de Wolfe

5. Don't Feel Compelled to Fill Up All the Spaces

Space is a luxury and having pure space gives us a serene feeling. Covering up every inch of space is suffocating. Respect architecture as a background for your private world of retreat. Enjoy the play of light and shadow that space permits. You shouldn't have to bruise your knee in a maze of overcrowding. No room requires seating for more than eight. When there are more people, they can stand or sit on folding chairs, depending on the occasion. Ottomans may be placed decoratively under a glass-topped coffee table, and brought out as required. Keep the four corners of the room clean and clear. Great rooms have free corners. Remember, decorators and home furnishing stores don't make money off bare space. However, you will feel less anxious and more at rest in a room that breathes with openness, like a refreshing walk in the country.

While a room requires backup storage areas for the paraphernalia of life, they can be cleverly disguised to keep the room from looking overcluttered. An armoire can add height and scale to a room while it hides a television, VCR, family scrapbooks, stationery, old magazines, or file folders. An end table can be a chest of drawers to store fine table linens. You can use a pine trunk for a coffee table. Try to avoid built-ins, which will make your rooms feel smaller, or paint them white (which helps fool the eye). Use imagination to solve your storage requirements.

6. Don't Make a Room a Stage Set

Down with pretense, sham, aesthetic quackery, up with honesty, sincerity.
—Charles Locke Eastlake, Hints on Household Taste, *1870*

When a living room is decorated to impress company, it fails for everyday living. Stage-set rooms look and feel artificial; successful rooms are alive with your vitality and personality and both of these come from *use*. Your living room is not meant only for entertaining guests. Friends want to be able to walk into the immediacy of your private world, and have your rooms generate energy and enthusiasm. Furniture and decorative objects alone can't do this. You have to live in rooms to have them appear lived in. Peter and I have received more compliments on our New York living room since we set up both our writing tables in it, placing one at each end. We didn't create a private living room to please others at the exclusion of our own pleasure. The more authentic a room, the more interesting. Show me where you "live." That will be the room I'll want to come to as your guest. Turn rarely used rooms into functioning spaces for daily living and you will achieve a far more charming atmosphere for others.

7. Experiment with Light

Most rooms, unhappily, are dark and dreary. When a room doesn't have enough light, it dampens the spirit, making you feel

tired and sad. Being inside our houses and apartments with ordinary lamplight gives us only 10 percent of the natural light we
would enjoy from being outside on a summer afternoon. Light
the lights. Light candles. Install a dimmer switch so you can
control your lamps. Just as we need light to read by and in order
to feel cheerful, paintings and objects need to be highlighted, too.
Light your shelves with low-wattage incandescent bulbs and
hang decorative picture lights over your paintings. Avoid fluorescent lighting whenever possible: Studies show that it produces
anxiety. Beware of the humming sound of some halogen lamps.
When making your lighting selections, go to the store and spend
the time you would if you were buying a pair of shoes. Try them
on—turn them on. Even with overhead lighting, it is nice to have
lamps on tables and standing lamps in seating areas. It's the close
proximity to light that makes us feel cozy.

8. Do Not Exclude Nature

Rooms that don't breathe fresh air seem claustrophobic. Create a color scheme inspired by nature. Think of the color green
as grass, of blue as sky and water, of yellow as sunshine. Always
have something growing in your rooms, even if it is a modest
basket arrangement of flowers from the garden. When you tend
your houseplants, your wood furniture seems more organically
alive, especially when we remember that all of our wooden furniture were once trees. Windows bring the outside in. Clean windows are like a cloudless day. White window trim intensifies
light. Wallpapers with vines, flowers, trees and outdoor scenes
are popular for all these reasons. Just as nature provides seasonal changes, so can our rooms. The more our rooms remind
us of the out-of-doors, the more they will solace as well as stim-
ulate us with natural beauty.

*We must have
beauty around us to
make us good.
—M.E.W.
Sherwood,
grandmother of the
playwright Robert
Sherwood*

9. Avoid the Errors of "Cutsie, Cutsie" and "Matchy-Matchy"

We all suffer from a tendency to accumulate sentimental objects that clutter every inch of surface space. There is no need to display our possessions all at once. Think of your knickknacks as costume jewelry. You can bring them out on occasion, but not too often is even better. "Cutsie, cutsie" are weeds that choke your garden. Dolls and stuffed animals seem more appropriate in a child's room than in a living room. Avoid displaying ashtrays from your travels and mementos, like little animals and statues, purchased from holiday gift shops. Be cautious with needlework pillows that have slogans or messages. We all have our toys. We could do as we did as children and bring them out only for special play times! (Cuckoo clocks make me especially crazy!) If you're a collector—of teapots, antique cups and saucers, figurines, china dolls, whatever—display your possessions with economy. I have a client who "puts up" her accumulated "cutsie, cutsie" every few months.

Remember, too, our homes are not hotel suites. Nothing is duller than everything being paired off—bedroom end tables that match the headboard, the headboard that matches the highboy; the dining room table that matches the chairs; and the chairs that match the sideboard. When everything is matched, the effect is stultifying. A room is far more interesting when it has a variety of woods, shapes, and textures. It's all right to have two identical chairs in a room, but they don't have to be placed symmetrically opposite each other. A dining room can successfully incorporate upholstered chairs with a wood table, or the table and chairs can be of contrasting woods. A pair of sofa tables shouldn't be identical. Two unmatched tables can be unified with a pair of lamps. Break up the boredom of the obvious with surprise touches. Every room can stand a touch of black or red lacquer. Have one intensely colored piece of porcelain in the room. Introduce an

Suitability is the quality that makes things durable.
—Billy Baldwin

object that is whimsical—a child's chair or a clay hand print from kindergarten. Remember, decorating is creative, and our best results are achieved not only through trial and error, but through combination and recombination.

10. Forget Rigid Rules and Follow Your Heart Instead

You may have read that coffee tables are approximately seventeen inches high, but that tea tables are higher. I have a petite painted French provincial desk in front of a loveseat in my bedroom. I find it a charming place to sit, make telephone calls, and sip morning coffee. In essence, I am using a loveseat as a chair and a desk as a coffee table. If you have two low Oriental-style tables, try stacking one on top of the other to make a coffee table. Basic principles guide us and give us confidence in making decorating decisions just as grammar gives order to our writing. However, the odd touch, the creative flair in prose as well as in personal style, is what makes what you write, or where you live, your unique signature.

SYNERGISM: BETWEEN YOU AND THE PEOPLE YOU HIRE

Decorating is an act of creation, but it is also a business for the people you will involve in successfully implementing your vision. You may choose to work with an interior designer, and or you may elect to go your own way. Nonetheless, you will invariably employ the services of independent contractors—whether they be electricians, masons, plumbers, tile setters, carpenters, wallpaper hangers, painters, or drapery installers. You are not an island. It's what goes on between you and these others that will help you execute your design schemes.

Many business transactions are oral. This arrangement works, however, only if both people who enter into an agreement

Identifies, researches and creatively solves problems pertaining to the function and quality of the interior environment. —description of a designer, National Council for Interior Design Qualification

are trustworthy. There is a strong tendency, especially in these litigious and recession-bound days, to ignore our obligations when the bill is presented. Everyone, regardless of profession, wants and expects to be paid what is owed for work that is done well, no matter how tight someone else's cash flow might be. In my opinion, it is wrong and unprofessional to allow your bills to go unpaid longer than sixty days. If you're going to assume financial obligations, be responsible and pay promptly. The respect you show toward those you have engaged mirrors the self-respect and pleasure you take in the results.

Overspending causes anxiety, so it is unwise to bite off more than you can chew. Budget less than you want to spend and be aware that it is perfectly possible that you will have to spend more. Estimates are *only* guesses. We professionals estimate what we think a job will cost, but until a job is under way, no one can really know the full extent of what's involved structurally and/or aesthetically. The only way to ensure that you don't lose money on an estimate is to build in an extra contingency amount of approximately 15 percent.

Be realistic about how much you'll have to spend. If you have unrealistic expectations about the actual prices for goods and services, you will frustrate yourself into thinking that someone is trying to rip you off or that something is outrageous. Whether or not the price of a yard of chintz is ridiculous, the price is nonnegotiable. While it is human nature to look for a deal and want a bargain, it is shortsighted to complain once you have agreed to pay the quoted price. If you are unhappy with the way a job has been completed, don't hesitate to speak up. All professionals stand behind their work and will make every attempt to satisfy a reasonable client.

Common sense and the Golden Rule apply to all money matters. If you are buying an object, you will pay the price if you feel comfortable with it, and if you don't, pass up the item and move on to a more appropriate purchase. Our homes require a

I try to design rooms around their architecture or to create architecture where none exists.
—Eleanor McMillen Brown

different kind of investment than the stock market or other business deals. Here, in your home, where you are called upon to express yourself emotionally, you may choose to engage a professional to help you fulfill it. Remain open to his/her ideas—but don't allow yourself to be intimidated. You know more than you think you do. Before you can trust someone else, trust yourself.

To buy or not to buy an object—a sofa, a chair, a lamp, a rug, an armoire, a painting, a mantel, a chandelier, a pair of curtains, a piece of porcelain, a quilt, a vase—requires a personal choice. You are free to make a selection based on preference. But if you have hired someone to advise you, so that choices will go together and be appropriate, you must be prepared to pay for the object as well as the service. Many interior decorators and designers make their money only at the point of purchase. Designers buy an object wholesale and sell it retail, and their gross profit, or fee, is the difference between these prices. Their net profit depends on what their discount is, what their overhead is, and on taxes. Tradespeople, in turn, will submit an estimate based on time and materials and overhead. Whomever you are hiring, interview the person carefully. Ask lots of questions, and check references. You may find that the cheapest person might not be the right one for you.

When Peter and I had saved up enough money to have the outside of our house painted, we asked our contractor to help us get some bids. The first painter we interviewed chewed gum, acted bored, and made me feel as though our house wasn't good enough for his company. He removed the keys to his truck from his pocket and went over to the side of our house and vigorously scratched off some paint. As he demonstrated the rotten condition of the exterior paint job of our 217-year-old house, he recommended removing all the clapboards and replacing them with plastic look-alikes. I thanked him and told him the reason we had bought the old house was to fix it up and restore it, but not to do anything to harm its original integrity. "We have no inten-

If you have marvelous taste and know exactly what you want, you don't need a decorator.
—Billy Baldwin

tion of replacing our clapboards," I told him, without hesitation. Peter and I both had bad vibrations about this man. We told our contractor not to have him bid on our job because we didn't want him to touch our dear old house.

While it is possible that someone we're considering hiring to help us with our home may have an excellent reputation for doing good work, this is not always enough. We need to like, respect, and trust that person implicitly. When we do, we can sit back, listen to their advice, and embrace their help. If someone in an advisory position suggests that you spend more money than you had planned, don't assume they have an ulterior motive. Listen and trust, then decide. When clients ask me, "What do you think?" I try to analyze their situation to the best of my knowledge, based on my ability and experience. However, I am often asked, "What would you do, Alexandra?" Then I answer them subjectively. If I sense that they are dying for me to persuade them to go for it, I usually do—if I am certain they can afford it financially and that they are making an appropriate choice. It's good to remember that people who work in service aren't out to take advantage of you. They *want* your repeat business—and your referrals.

Far away there in in the sunshine are my highest aspirations. I may not reach them, but I can look up and see their beauty, believe in them, and try to follow where they lead.
—Louisa May Alcott

E WILL BE "SURPRISED BY JOY" John Keats was right when he observed, "A thing of beauty is a joy forever." The external, intangible qualities of beauty and character that make up our home will reward us with pleasurable feelings and deep satisfactions day after day.

As we move now to explore your house room by room, remember that we are on this journey together. We will gain strength and comfort from each other and from the joy we will take from the art of creation. Creating a beautiful home is a personal adventure, but the pleasure comes from understanding that we all do this privately, under our own roof, in our own way. Everything we do at home can take on greater meaning. Just the other day, I was standing at the kitchen sink and the sun came out after a hard rain. Everything glistened and the light was blinding, reflecting off the white porcelain sink, full of rainbow bubbles. I looked up, and right in front of me were the lilac trees that first made me fall in love with the house in full bloom after the heavy rain, dripping now with teardrop diamonds of water. I wiped my hands on a cool, blue and white striped hand towel, went outside, and, so moved by the beauty, I began to cry. I was then, as I still am, surprised by joy. I cut off a few sprigs of white lilac, put them in an old majolica teapot and placed it on the kitchen farm table. This entire process took less than five minutes, but it will be a treasured memory forever.

This kind of joy happens all the time at home.

Part 2

CREATING YOUR

BEAUTIFUL HOME

Chapter 5

ENTRANCES

From the moment you open the front door to your house or apartment, you instinctively feel the emotional rush of being home. The entrance hall is the face and character of the house. Just as a writer must find his or her voice, your place of entry—like the first paragraph of a book—conveys the whole feel of the house, its atmosphere and integrity, the voice that hints of home.

Immediately, you reveal your story. So begin by asking, What are your major messages? What do you want to express to yourself, your family, and friends when walking through the door?

Most of us have given little thought to these questions because we use our front doors so rarely. Certainly, you want the front hall to invite people inside. You want your guests to know you expect them and that you care. You want them to know they are welcome.

In terms of everyday living, however, we have tended to make our front entrances obsolete. My mother pointed out to me long ago that people entered houses through the front door only at funeral receptions and weddings. Today, it's customary to enter our houses through the back door, or the cellar door, whichever is nearest the garage—convenient for carrying in groceries

If you get it right the first time, there is no need to change.
—Eleanor McMillen Brown

and other bundles, yes, but not exactly a gracious way to re-freshen our spirits after long hours away from home.

Perhaps it's because we've gotten away from putting our front entrances to daily use that so many of them feel stiff and awkward. If nothing else, I think it's time to rethink the daily pattern of entering our real lives through the back door. We should begin now to enjoy the full bounty of our houses every day.

As you begin to consider ways of preparing and energizing this space, start at the front door itself. If you haven't walked through it for a while, try it! Experience it from the outside in, the way your friends do. Feast your eye on your staircase. Look around you. Keep the front door open and let the light flood into the hall. Is your hall more formal than the rest of the house? Is the hall uplifting to you when you enter and walk through to adjoining rooms? If the floor gets filthy with normal use, then possibly it can be made more practical. Check to be sure your doormat works. If it is sisal, it will wear out every year or so.

Your front entrance hall floor should actually be the most dramatic one in your house because it's the first thing people see. If the floor is hardwood, you might think about bleaching and staining it to create interest. Peter and I did this in our New York apartment. We were fortunate to have oak floors with a chevron design concealed under a black-and-white vinyl floor that had been laid in another life. Because the hall is put to so many different uses, we can't accommodate a rug. So we created a zigzag design, outlining the floorboards by bleaching some and using masking tape where we didn't want the stain to touch. Then we stained the remaining floorboards a walnut brown. Our floor has a lot of warmth and style, as well as being extremely practical. We put a thin coat of polyurethane over the stain and then applied some clear Butcher's paste wax. The floor gets heavy wear and tear from normal daily traffic through the apart-

Man has moved through the long passages of time digesting, recording, changing, but always leaving in his time and place the records of how he lived and why.
—Eleanor McMillen Brown

ment, but it's easy to care for and gives a special look to our long entrance hall.

It's also a good idea to coordinate the floors of the adjacent rooms with your entrance hall floor. The last thing you want is your off-white wall-to-wall living room carpet to become tracked with grass and mud stains from the outdoors. Consider your entrances fully before you invest in rugs that can't tolerate the foot marks of family and friends coming through.

As you analyze your hall, take stock of its shape and size: Most entrance halls tend to be quite narrow. Consider its light sources, the color of the woodwork and ceiling, its furniture and architectural detail. Is the staircase visible from the front door? Do you put your mail on a front hall table? Does the table hold a plant or have a place for flowers?

Quite possibly, your front hall already has architectural features that give it personality; but if it lacks character, consider installing a thick cornice molding (found at your local lumberyard) where the wall touches the ceiling. Perhaps you can add a more interesting baseboard. If the existing trim around the door is too narrow, it can be replaced by a thick molding. Columns, too, can be used for architectural distinction as well as to create special drama where none exists. For instance, friends opened up their apartment's tiny entranceway by replacing the living room and dining room walls at either side with decorative columns, which gives an impression of sweeping grandeur while also practically preserving the separation of their living and dining spaces.

City living, in fact, presents tricky decorating problems for entrances. Because they are often long and narrow, installing a mirror on a narrow wall often creates a sense of expanded space and brings in light. I also encourage my city clients always to have fresh flowers or a flowering plant on the front hall table, or a bowl of apples, lemons, limes, and oranges. But because most entrance halls don't get enough natural light, plants and

In our modern industrial society it is the professional designer who increasingly is determining the appearance of our physical environment.
— Arthur A. Houghton

flowers will require rotation to and from a sunny window ledge. We grow geraniums and narcissus at our New York kitchen window and bring them into the hall to enjoy. Having something colorful from nature livens up a hall.

Of course, many entrances feel dark — city and country alike. After being outside in the light, we don't want to come home only to immediately feel caged in. When you come home at night, you want to feel comforted by a light, cheerful atmosphere. So I recommend airy, bright entrances — whites or yellows and high-gloss enamel trims; yellow is excellent for entranceways because the color smiles at you, suggesting sunlight. Dark woodwork or paneling absorbs light. Unless these walls are truly handsome, consider painting them. When I worked on an eighteenth-century farmhouse in Rhode Island, I suggested that my clients bleach the beams, which had darkened over the centuries.

Once you've examined your entrances from the point of view of light, size, and proportion, you will be ready to dress them. An entrance hall — just like any other space in your home — need not be a static stage set, indifferently decorated or unlived in and unused. I'm increasingly disenchanted with the rigid formality I see all too often in this room. If a hall doesn't have some whimsy and individuality, it feels inflexible and cold.

When my mind flashes back to some of my favorite entrance halls, I realize they all partake of the warmth and personality of their owners: a boot rack and riding crops in the front hall of a gentleman's farm in Louisville, Kentucky. Terra-cotta pots filled with tulips massed under a stairwell of a Fort Lauderdale home. And a charming Cape Cod cottage features a playful hooked rug especially designed for the family to reflect all their interests: a tennis racquet; their Irish setter, Gille; their cat, Flash; colorful flowers from their gardens; and their sailboat. This active family's spirit was well represented in this small masterpiece.

I love our small, simple Connecticut hall. In it we have a rustic seventeenth-century rectangular oak bench stacked with

The essence of taste is suitability.
—Edith Wharton,
French Ways and Their Meanings

some of our favorite quilts, which turned out to be an excellent way to infuse the space with splashes of vibrant color and to establish a theme repeated throughout the house. Peter and I are inveterate quilt collectors, and we have them everywhere. Underneath the bench is another collection—duck decoys, which Peter has carried back from his travels across California, Illinois, and Long Island. Another favorite front hall possession is an old English letterbox; my warm affinity for letters makes this handsome object rich with sentimentality. The spirit of our house is informality. So we have a bare floor in our hall, with a small, flowered hooked rug by the front door. The pine stair treads, immediately visible from the front door, are also bare, but at the top of the steps to the second floor is a nineteenth-century folk art white swan. Behind the swan, on the wall, is a yellow and white crib quilt of sailboats. Our entrance hall hardly makes a sophisticated statement, but it expresses how we live with our family and greet our friends.

OTHER ENTRANCES

When you park the car in the garage and walk through the back door, what do you see? One client saw her washer-dryer and laundry gear and decided to conceal them with a hand-painted folding screen. The screen, painted by a friend, was lightweight and portable, allowed light to come into the hall from the window above the machines, yet still hid the utilitarian equipment. A back hall (or laundry area) doesn't have to be grubby or look like a locker room.

Pretend that your back entrance is your front hall. Keep it simple and straightforward, but give it some charm. If stairs can be seen from your back door, paint the treads a bright color—red, green, yellow, or blue—and stencil the risers. We used a grass-green color for the treads on our back stairs, and the risers

I was flying homeward now . . . to books, to music, refinement, company, pleasure, and the dear old homestead I love so well.
—Sybylla Melvyn,
My Brilliant Career

are painted bright white. On the walls, we have started to group family photographs, which are framed in a variety of different styles and colors.

We also turned our back hall into a reference room that opens into a snug, warm study. Space is there to manipulate! When we use the study, this hall forms a natural extension of it and lends richness to a small, otherwise useless space. It would be terrific to have a mud room, or a potting shed, or a space to fold laundry, but we have enjoyed creating an illusion of spaciousness in an area that could easily have been ignored.

Create rooms within rooms.

I have a theory about houses. The front is the most formal and correct. The middle loosens up a bit after we've passed through our public rooms into our private, intimate rooms. By the time we get to the back, there is children's art on the walls, good smells coming from the kitchen, and there is laughter. No matter how your house is arranged, don't feel obligated to maintain this public-versus-private division. If you enjoy formality, then it will be reflected in all the decisions you make throughout the house. But if you want a more relaxed feeling, utilize your entrances to achieve this goal.

GRACE NOTES

◼ The front door says welcome. It is the first and last thing we see going in and out. Paint it high-gloss white, French blue, canary yellow, or New England barn red, on the exterior only. Inside, the door will be white to match the trim.

◼ Make your entry hall a focal point. Analyze it carefully and let it establish the spirit of your home. All entrances should create a special atmosphere.

◼ If your hall is long, consider mirroring one wall to give illusion of a wider room. Install a mirror over a chair rail or one that goes down to the baseboard. Have the mirror installer cut the panel heights to line up with the tops of the door trims. If you require more than one panel, break up the width of the walls in three sheets. Only use clear mirror.

▦ Analyze your hall. Walk through it as though you were a guest. Jot down your immediate impressions. If you do this after you've been away on vacation, you'll see everything with fresh eyes.

▦ If your hall isn't to be used for other purposes, it might have a colorful rug that is welcoming. Perhaps you could hook your own colorful rag rug, using favorite fruits and vegetables in the design. The Ruggery, in Glen Cove, Long Island, can send you the canvas and natural vegetable-dyed yarns for the rug. The firm will also do a drawing. If you wish, they'll hook your rug for you.

▦ Every hall needs a table or a bench with stacks of quilts on it for warmth and color. In our apartment hall, there is a large table we use for eating.

▦ If the hall is large enough for a table, keep a pretty basket for your mail, messages, and fresh flowers on it. I love to sit at our hall table, open mail, write notes, and talk on the telephone.

▦ To use the hall as a home office, just have the phone company install a jack inside the hall closet with a 25-foot cord so you can plug in a telephone. Consider using half your hall closet for files and stationery supplies. Most halls are too dark. Install ceiling lighting, either track lights, a lantern, or recessed can lights, as well as a decorative lamp on the table. To add drama, put a can lighting fixture on the floor to flood light up toward the ceiling.

▦ If you use your hall as a dining area and your table is large, a pair of lamps can be used. When Peter and I eat in the hall, we keep the lamps on the table.

▦ If you have a staircase in your front hall, don't be in a rush to cover it with carpeting. Paint the risers and the spindles semi-gloss white enamel. Match the wood of the steps to a tone in your hall floor. Stain the banister a compatible brown tone.

▦ If you choose to have a carpet runner on the stairs, leave at least a 4-inch margin on either side of the runner to show polished wood and gleaming white paint.

▦ A small, lively rug on the floor as you step into the hall is like a welcome mat. Because the area gets a lot of traffic, the background should be a medium color so the dirt won't show.

▦ Lettuce green is always a good background tone for a hall rug because it brings nature inside.

▦ If you own a set of watercolors of botanicals or birds, they will look charming hung on the wall next to the stairs. If you have pastel sketches of your children, that is a wonderful place for them also.

▦ The hall is a great place to hang a favorite painting because then you and everyone else see it coming and going.

▦ Don't use wall sconces, unless they are beautiful, because they never give off enough light.

▦ Hinges and knobs are like jewelry. They add style and elegance to a door. Hardware can be lacquered to eliminate the need for polishing.

▦ Your entrances should be attractive as well as useful. If there's more than one entrance to your house or apartment, walk through each door and evaluate what you see.

▦ The main entryway to your house should immediately reveal your personality. Make the same decisions here that you do in the heart of your home. If you have folk art in the family room, you can also have it in the entrance area.

▦ Hang a quilt on the wall. Sew Velcro on the top length of the quilt. Staple Velcro to a 2-inch-wide wood lattice strip to the wall with 1-inch-long brads. Then put up the quilt.

▦ Select useful furniture for your hall, such as a chest of drawers to hold scarves and gloves. A table with a drawer can house postcards, stationery, stamps, and mailing envelopes. A table can also be used for mail, keys, and notes.

▦ Decide whether you want to have a hall rug or not. If you prefer not to have a decorative rug, the hall floor can be of a different material than the other floors, such as brick, tile, stone, or marble.

▦ All doors lead somewhere. Treat each door the same way so that there is repetition of scale and design, which creates harmony.

▦ Paint the woodwork and doors semi-gloss white enamel. This paint is white-white, and will pick up the tones of the walls. You can use the same white throughout the house.

▦ Paint the trim with high-gloss, white enamel, oil-based paint to make the room sparkle. This paint is so white that it reflects the surrounding colors in the glow.

▦ Yellow is an excellent entrance color because it brings the sunny cheerfulness of the out-of-doors into a space where there aren't as many windows as other rooms of the house. Consider using Perfect Yellow, Fuller O'Brien 1-A-78.

▦ Semi-gloss walls are easy to maintain and they reflect light.

▦ To clean dirt marks from the walls and trim use Formula 409 on a clean cotton rag.

▦ Mirrors expand space. Hang a decorative mirror in the entryway to show off some attractive features on the opposite wall. The center of the mirror should be at eye level when you stand.

▦ To add architectural style, consider adding pediments to the tops of your doors. Study the most beautiful old houses for inspiration.

▦ If the wood of the floor has a chevron design, you can create a zigzag pattern by bleaching one row, staining the next, then bleaching two rows and staining two rows, repeating this process, using three rows of each, and then going back to one row of bleach and stain. Cover the areas you want to keep light with masking tape.

▦ To create a country-style feeling, you can stencil the floor. Scrape the wood. Decide what color you want the floor to be. You can buy aniline stains in many different colors. You might choose a medium green and a stencil design that is a darker green.

▦ Try ragging your walls. If you paint the walls a flat color— say Pistachio Green, Fuller O'Brien 1-F-11—put some semi-gloss enamel white on a clean piece of chamois cloth and dab the walls. When it dries, the white will sparkle.

▦ Select something amusing to put in your hall: a hat rack, a boot holder, a child's wooden rocking horse, a bin of old walking cancs, or a group of old duck decoys on the floor. There should be some surprises to greet you and your friends.

▦ Have something from nature in your entrance: flowers from the garden, a flowering geranium plant in a terra-cotta pot, a basket of apples or some lemons in a porcelain bowl on the hall table.

▦ Install a dimmer switch for your overhead lighting.

▦ Have your lamps on a three-way switch to alter the mood.

▦ Light a candle in the evening to welcome family, friends, and guests.

▦ Keep the entrance lights on to add a glow to the inside of your house at night.

▦ Have a guest book for everyone to sign before they leave.

Chapter 6

THE LIVING ROOM

*L*iving rooms have always had a disproportionate amount of money spent on them because people tended to think they had to be "decorated." Yet no sooner was the (expensive) work completed than the living room ceased to be a room lived *in*; we'd glide past it on our way to the sitting room or kitchen or bedroom or den, where we could really feel good. While our domestic lives unfolded elsewhere around the house, this room remained off limits. The stiffness of the decor; the dark, forbidding grains of the woods; the rigid seating arrangements; the bric-a-brac and dim lighting screamed to our senses: KEEP OUT! because the formal room was reserved for special occasions, and the daily ordinariness of family life was not considered "special."

Today, everything has changed. We don't decorate our living rooms anymore. Our *living* decorates them. Slowly, we came to realize we were approaching our homes in the wrong way, and gained confidence in our appreciation that successful living rooms are finally visual metaphors of our good living.

Where do people literally live anyway? When we are at home, studies show, approximately 96 percent of our time is

Make every room a living room.

❖

9 5

spent alone or with our family—but only 4 percent of that home time is spent in company. This is all the more reason to create a living room that you will really put to use. Certainly, you want the room to be charming and to look wonderful, but your aspirations will be achieved only if you privately love being there. If the room is set up for your comfort, it will effortlessly and naturally expand to meet the requirements of your guests also. When a room is designed for intimate living, it doesn't matter if it's two or twenty you need to accommodate. The best living rooms never make artificial statements; they simply reveal their owners' personal signature.

Some of my favorite living rooms are actually quite simple and unornamented. I am reminded of an Austin, Texas, room that had a bare, pickled-pine floor, laid down on a diagonal, with blue and white canvas slipcovered sofas and a free-standing antique pine bar with high stools. A striking wall quilt of blue, yellow, and watermelon red complemented the colors of the sofas' cotton throw pillows and the fresh flowers in a coffee table vase. And I remember a Chicago apartment, high above Lake Michigan, with its natural sisal living room rug, its dark green, leaf-designed, woven-textured wool upholstery and dark mahogany furniture. The room's curtains were white cotton cloth and were hung on simple white poles.

Whether you use exuberant chintzes or old Pendleton plaids on your upholstered pieces, needlework pillows or sailcloth, an educated mix of antique, reproduction, or contemporary pieces on which to display framed family photographs and other favorite objects, you can create a living space at reasonable cost that makes *everyone* feel comfortable, that connects comfortably to the rest of your rooms, and that celebrates itself as the focal point of your daily life.

Begin by determining if you are satisfied structurally with the room. Perhaps the room can benefit by the removal of an old ceiling to expose its structural beams, which can then be stained or washed in a bath of fresh white paint. An enlarged living room

Let's be honest about it. That big room isn't the living room at all. Unless you have a great many rooms, that is a ghastly waste of space. The living room should be lived in.
—*Billy Baldwin*

doorway can make a dramatic difference to an otherwise modestly proportioned space, or French doors or fanlight windows can be installed to give an impression of Old World charm. Sometimes, too, you can create the illusion of a grander space simply by linking together two small rooms using good old-fashioned paint.

This is precisely what we did in our Connecticut house. The living room is actually two small square rooms separated by an 8-foot-wide archway that originally framed a pair of doors closing off these front and rear spaces. One room had a view of the water, but a nonworking fireplace; the other had a huge wood-burning fireplace, ideal to curl up in front of to read and enjoy conversation on winter days and evenings, but no view. Because we wanted our living room to combine both features—the view and the fire—we made a larger room without altering the architecture by painting the walls and woodwork fresh white. This solution not only increased the physical dimension of the space but also its visual appearance. Immediately, the two areas came together.

Your walls can also be manipulated to make a large room appear more intimate, refined, or charming, just as they can make a small space feel more expansive. Just think of the walls as the horizon of your living room's landscape and make them clear and refreshing. You may select a pleasant, neutral color that can be enlivened by semi-gloss or high-gloss paint to make the walls shine, or add a chair rail, a hand-stenciled border molding, or even a faux sponged finish to make the walls more interesting.

One decision dictates the next. Because light is especially important to me, we knew we wanted to carry our white walls through to our window treatment. What were our options? At first, I toyed with the idea of shutters, which are practical insofar as they take up no space, add architectural interest to most rooms, and allow light to come in while still preserving privacy. Ultimately, I decided they would be too heavy, too solid for this delicate little house, and instead I selected café curtains made

The art of living is a priceless achievement worth all the courage it requires.

from a white woven Swiss cotton in a stripe similar to a handkerchief. The curtains are hung two to a window on white wooden dowels, so that the bottom curtains can be closed for privacy from the street and the top ones left open to bring in as much daylight as possible. This curtain treatment is in fact repeated on all the windows throughout the house, with the exclusion of an upstairs sitting room where the curtain fabric is actually simple blue and white kitchen dish towels.

You, too, will probably want your living room to have as much light and sunshine as possible. Study the quality of the natural light and judge how much your windows provide. What are your exposures? How many windows do you have, and how large are they? (The more windows, and the bigger they are, the more expensive they will be to cover — which may very well stop you in your tracks and direct you to a more simplified window treatment.) If you love curtains, then have beautiful windows warmed by materials you like. My only suggestion is that you keep the curtains straightforward. Elaborate window dressings — heavy draperies and valances — seem outdated in most rooms today and are expensive dust catchers. Also consider removing the original window hardware (this also applies to the door hardware throughout your house), which has most likely been painted many times over, and send them out to be cleaned and restored to their original shiny brass condition.

When deciding which curtain style to choose, consider what you want them to do for the room. If you want to add color, warmth, pattern, or spark to an awkward window situation, try straight-hanging lined panels with ample fullness (so they look generous) with an interesting heading (the way in which the material is gathered at the top to give it fullness). The most common heading is the French heading, also known as pinch pleats. Avoid this one. While you see it in most ready-made curtains, it looks ordinary. Examine all kinds of decorative headings before you settle on one (here again, magazines are particularly useful). You might also think about taking an entirely different route by

What's practical is beautiful. . . and suitability always overrules fashion.
—Billy Baldwin

using shades. Clients framed their simple living room windows by building pilasters (flat, upright architectural columns) and covering the windows with simple linen shades. Another client preferred to leave her apartment windows bare in order to effectively access the magnificent view of the cityscape below.

As you begin to focus on interior design, remember that all good rooms have a mission. In the case of your living room, its purpose and intent is to provide maximum emotional and physical comfort for you and your guests. What fascinates me as a decorator is not just the look of a room, but the way people respond when they're in that room. Do they seem relaxed? Are there certain areas that feel more inviting than others? Does the furniture arrangement encourage conversation and enhance communication? Does the room have a focal point, such as a fireplace or a wonderful view, around which you should arrange your main seating group? Does it contain a high piece on which to focus attention and draw you into the room?

Let your room grow slowly and build your furniture collection with thoughtful consideration of the need to feel relaxed and comfortable. Fight your impulse to crowd it with too much furniture; never buy anything just to fill the space, and remember that pieces that are beautifully designed and inviting can be harmoniously blended. When each single piece of furniture is superb in style and character and your eye has made the selection, all pieces will automatically go together and give the room a harmony of form and coordination. The simple lines of contemporary upholstery go in all rooms, in all settings. They complement that mellow old English secretary and fine decorative porcelain. In upholstery, smooth, straight, and simple lines make the most welcoming places to lounge. Check seat, arm, and back heights and repeat them often. Measure your sofa back to be certain it's low enough to "float" in your room and not have to be stuck against a wall.

Never create a single seating area for more than eight people. I have found that when more than eight are sitting together, the

When you arrange your living room furniture, think less of symmetry and more of comfort.
—Billy Baldwin

social gathering loses its feeling of intimacy and can become stiff and awkward. In fact, if possible, your living room should have at least two sitting areas—one large and one small, where two people can visit over tea or coffee. If the furniture in your main seating group has its back to the smaller one, it will act as a wall to create a feeling of privacy. In our New York apartment, some of the best conversations I've enjoyed with guests, or with my daughters, have been in the cozy far corners of the living room, where we have a yellow chintz-covered loveseat and two upholstered chairs on swivels.

We often hear the expression "Pull up a chair," but we can only do so if the chairs are movable. It's nice to have a few pull-up chairs (not too bulky or too heavy) or small ottomans or stools that can be spontaneously added to a grouping. Your furnishings should be flexible enough to offer comfort and intimacy and be easily adapted to all needs and occasions.

Applying this "magic of eight" to my Stonington living room was a challenge, remembering that we were attempting to harmonize two spaces successfully. We did so by using the same upholstery in both, all covered in a blue and white striped floral chintz pattern. The effect was of a mirror image, once again visually expanding the appearance of the rooms.

I placed two 5-foot-long loveseats opposite each fireplace. In the arch between the backs of the loveseats I put a 47-inch round French fruitwood table. I enjoy sitting there, in the center of both spaces, where I am able to see the fire as well as the view of the harbor and its often spectacular sunsets. I can write, read, or enjoy contemplative moments in this lovely spot.

My professional mentor, Mrs. Brown, taught me that repetition creates harmony. So I bought two pairs of matched upholstered swivel chairs (I am partial to these!) one on each side of both fireplaces and covered the four chairs in the same chintz as the loveseats, as well as a large ottoman that we move around as needed.

The main color in our room comes from this vibrant chintz

Stick to the things you really love. An honest room is always up to date.
—Billy Baldwin

❖

fabric. Your living room should be an uplifting space, and color can create a wonderful mood. I've been in some thrilling dark-colored living rooms and admire them enormously; but for me, the effect is like the difference between going to the mountains or going to the sea. Decide which type you are and select the colors that reflect the spirit you want to evoke. Try, however, to avoid "nothing" color; it will drown your lively colors of their energy. By "nothing" color, I do not mean "neutral"—since even within neutral tones there is a wide range. When choosing a color scheme, consider your light exposures. The soft green that looked great in someone else's house may be all wrong in yours if you have north light. Your favorite colors do not have to be blanketed about but might be reserved for a pillow, a coffee table, or a vase of flowers. Color contrast sharpens everything and also allows you the peace of focusing on one thing at a time.

There's nothing more fun than choosing our fabrics, and very often that's the decision we want to make first. But fabric choices often confound us. There are so many of them, one more beautiful than the next. And these of course must also be coordinated with your floor, wall, and window treatments. These are the most personal and subjective choices you will have to make, but when you do, make them with people in mind. The best way to bring "life" into your living room is to use warm, soft, practical textures and materials. Fragile fabrics such as silk brocade create rigidity; choose thick fabrics that are beautifully made for wear and tear and thinner materials (that are cleanable) for accents. Remember, too, that fabrics are often discontinued; so if you can, purchase an extra bolt in case you need to re-cover your upholstered pieces down the road. (I stored my New York living room fabric underneath my sofa and was glad I did ten years later when I had to recover two very used chairs!)

Ask yourself: Do you prefer your pattern (or texture) in your rug, accessories, and wall decorations, or in your upholstery? If you are drawn to chintz, as I am, study examples carefully and pick one you won't tire of. Unless you "know it when you see

There is no reason, either in prose or in rhyme, why a whole house should not be a poem.
—Ella Church Rodman

it" and flip for one exciting material, try another tack. For instance, you can create interest in a room without having dominant patterns in your fabrics, through a material's weave and texture, and through the combination of many color tonalities. Paintings and books also bring in a lot of pattern. For an artist client who displays her own paintings, I was able to use woven textures in shades of lilac, silver, and plum to complement the palette of her artwork.

Similarly, use your flooring to create or sustain the room's mood. To me, there is nothing more beautiful than bare, freshly waxed hardwood floors, and both my New York and Connecticut living rooms are unusual in that the floors are completely uncovered. Many people, however, like to enhance the beauty of their floors by spreading rugs in key areas to articulate a seating arrangement and to create intimacy and warmth. Rugs help to define a given area and bring a furniture group together. Whether you use Oriental rugs, Indian dhurries, or braided, hooked, or other contemporary rugs, do your research and compare prices. Interesting handmade modern rugs are often like works of art and can be as expensive as some of the old ones. Look around until you find one that you love. The color of your rug is what everything else rests on.

A successful room must strike just the right balance between upholstered and wooden furniture. When you fill up your rooms with too much of either, or both, you diminish the meaning of each individual piece. Once we had settled on our upholstered pieces in Connecticut, the wood furniture fell into place naturally—beginning with that high Swedish cabinet originally intended for our upstairs sitting room. What we at first cursed as poor luck turned out to be a stroke of serendipity, because the cabinet introduced scale as well as height into a space that needed a note of surprise to break up the repetition of the matching shapes and upholstery pattern.

The other furniture in this room consists of small desks, which we use as end tables; Windsor, ladderback, and corner

Repeat shapes to gain harmony.
—Eleanor McMillen Brown

chairs; and a weaver's bench and several stools. One coffee table had once been a Chinese bench used for tea ceremonies; the other coffee table is actually a seventeenth-century joint oak stool. Coffee tables, in fact, offer all kinds of opportunities for creative risk-taking, because they are an invention of modern times. Don't be afraid to be imaginative!

Our most prominent decorative accents are a raspberry and white appliqué American quilt and one that is blue and white, each slung casually across the sofa backs. Lamps, too, are important decorative accessories, and indeed may even be thought of as sculpture. In our case, we decided to buy some hand-painted faïence vase lamps made in Brittany from friends who live in our village and own a shop on our street. We felt pleased that these "peasant ware" lamps fit so well with both our color scheme and the spirit of our cottage.

Lamps, of course, are necessary as well as decorative, but should never be thought of as replacements for natural sunlight. Your living room isn't necessarily a *night* room; this is your home, after all, not a nightclub. Your daytime lighting should always come from the outside in.

In the evening, it is better to have many different sources of illumination bathing the room instead of just a few lights of high wattage. There is nothing romantic or chic about ceiling lighting in a living room. It is just a way to get your room lighted, but it should never be regarded as complete in and of itself. Rather, use a variety of arrangements so that the mood of the room can change continually. Table lamps with three-way bulbs; dimmers; standing lamps with glass, brass, or chrome shades; and sconces all provide efficient as well as aesthetically pleasing ways to manipulate room lighting according to your needs at any given moment.

Our living room has evolved and become even more meaningful to us as we have moved around our paintings and decorative objects. Our personal treasures are the appointments that set our rooms apart, filling them with warmth and personality.

Opulent comfort
—Sister Parish

Heirloom china plates, framed family photographs—even the dreaded white elephants, such as that awful ceramic figurine you received from your husband's favorite aunt as a wedding present—these accessories can act as a visual autobiography of you and your family.

The key to making the most of your favorite objects is to display them in creative ways, grouping certain treasures together while paring down others. The mantel of one living room fireplace for instance displays our porcelain trompe-l'oeil fruit and vegetable collection, while the other has an assortment of brass candlesticks and carriage clocks. We have a grouping of brass banks and little boxes, a bell with a wooden handle, and a magnifying glass resting on top of the room's large center table. Small paintings on easels, colorful beeswax candles in hurricane globes, and modest bouquets of cut flowers decorate our end tables and coffee tables.

You'll be surprised how interesting any collection of objects, no matter how quirky, can appear when thoughtfully and stylishly displayed. A friend purchased an old glass curio cabinet for a collection of tiny beaded purses and petit-point handbags that once belonged to her grandmother. Another friend has placed a beautiful antique English dollhouse, found at a country fair, on the table behind her sofa, while a client created an elegant sculpture of cut-crystal decanters filled with sherry, port, and Lillet, and colorful Venetian cordial glasses, all arranged on a silver tray on her coffee table.

When creating your own collections, look for common denominators. Your treasures should be compatible in at least one way, whether it be subject, theme, shape, texture, or color. When grouping photographs, keep the black-and-white ones together and the color portraits separately. And while it's wonderful to display family pictures in a variety of frames, they should be similar in style and/or material—silver, wood, metal, and so on. Finally, change your displays frequently so they keep looking

*The reason for having taste is to increase one's faculties for enjoyment.
—Russell Lynes*

fresh to you. Keep in mind that some objects work best during certain seasons. I like to bring out my brass and silver objects in the darker fall and winter months to give my rooms more of a glow.

Our accessories bridge hundreds of miles and years, evoke strong feelings of memories past, fill us with pleasure, and make us feel at home in our living spaces. We have to "wear in" a room much like we do a bathrobe or a pair of new shoes, and we should always be ready to rethink the room as the structure of our life changes.

As you work toward your goals, remember that your living room is not meant to be simply admired by your guests, but shared. Make this room become a space that you, your spouse, and children can claim for yourselves, and allow it to become a personal sanctuary in which you can catch a quiet moment to enjoy the things that you love—natural light, flowers, books, art, and music—to daydream and nap in, to replenish the spirit, and as a constant resource from which to draw nourishment and sustenance.

It's more amusing to mix things up. I like all periods.
—Gary Hager, decorator

❖

GRACE NOTES

❖ The living room is not for guests only, but should be set up as a useful, practical area where you spend a large part of your time.

❖ Paint all trim semi-gloss enamel white. This paint is a superior pigment that is pure, and picks up reflections of all the surrounding colors.

❖ Determine what your focal point will be. If you don't have a fireplace, consider a high piece to focus your attention and draw you into the room.

✳ Let your room grow slowly. Don't crowd it with too much furniture. Let the space "breathe."

✳ One of the most important pieces of furniture will be a sofa. If the room is large, an 84-inch sofa that seats three people is ideal.

✳ Measure your room, locate the doors. Measure everything in inches to avoid mistakes. You can then convert the inches into feet later by adding machine.

✳ Keep a "Home" section in your personal notebook that goes with you wherever you are. This should include all measurements, paint chips, and fabric samples.

✳ Paint the ceiling flat Atmosphere Blue. Use full-color, Fuller O'Brien 1-0-47.

✳ Invest in a sturdy 12- to 25-foot Stanley Powerlock tape measure at your hardware store. Also buy a small 5-foot measuring tape to carry in your purse or briefcase at all times.

✳ Consider framing your watercolors using Solar Museum glass to protect them from fading in the light.

✳ When you buy an apartment or house, remove all old draperies, hooks, and carpeting to get a fresh start.

✳ One of the best furniture polishes is Goddard's Fine Furniture Polish with Almond Oil.

✳ Replace the facing of your fireplace with Vermont verde marble.

▦ Wherever you live, your room has two seasons. In the winter, your furniture grouping should be focused, inward, and cozy. In the summer, your furniture grouping should be open and airy with some pieces near the windows. Take up the winter rugs and put light slipcovers on the furniture.

▦ Do not overscale lamps. A 15-inch-high lamp base requires only an 11-inch lampshade. All of the lamps in my living room are 26 inches high, including the shade. A classic lampshade size: 8 inches top diameter, 11 inches deep, and 14 inches bottom diameter.

▦ Your coffee table can be large and still be in proportion to the sofa, as long as you allow approximately 19 inches at either end so people can move around it easily. Place the coffee table approximately 13 inches in front of the sofa.

▦ The depth of your upholstered sofa should be compatible with the depth of your upholstered chairs in order to keep them in scale. Check to be sure the seat height is the same for both. The average seat height for sofas and chairs is 18 inches.

▦ If at all possible, have two or more furniture groupings in the room. The more intimate, the better. First, determine where your main seating arrangement should be and then build from there, finding space for an additional grouping.

▦ No room should ever seat more than eight people in a grouping. When more people are gathered, they should either break up into several smaller groups, or some people should stand.

▦ Give your room some architectural details if needed. If the room doesn't have a cornice molding, you can select a simple one at your lumberyard. The cornice molding should connect the ceiling and the wall. Depending on the scale of the room and the height of the ceiling, this molding should be 3 to 6 inches deep.

▦ I prefer painted walls to wallpaper, especially in the living room. Paint is fresh and clean and allows you to hang paintings, prints, and quilts without a distracting background.

▦ Create a light, bright living room with white walls or a pale pastel yellow (Sunny Daisy, Fuller O'Brien, 1-A-22), peach (Hope 1-B-23), or pink (Pink Cream 1-C-22). Peter and I have pale pink walls in our living room.

▦ Have a glass company cut several 6-inch squares with a ¼-inch bevel to protect your table surfaces from moisture from flower vases.

▦ At your local lumberyard, select a simple molding for a chair rail. Paint it gloss enamel white. If you live in a house, be sure the linings of your curtains are not visible from the outside, and if they are, make sure they are decorative.

▦ An excellent source of lighting is a standing halogen lamp, which gives off the equivalent of 450 watts of light. This lamp comes with a dimmer switch. At their highest setting, halogen lamps can illuminate a 6-foot radius. The light is reflected off the ceiling.

▦ Use mirrors architecturally to increase the visual space of a room. If you intend to use large sheets of mirror, install a 2¼-inch chair rail approximately 32 inches from the floor so that the mirror actually rests on the molding.

▦ Welting (the cord in the seam of upholstery) can be in a contrasting color; for example, in a multicolored flowered chintz, you can pick up the dark green from the leaves of the flowers.

▦ Consider grouping a collection of antique boxes or baskets under a table.

▦ Remember, every tabletop gives you an opportunity to create a still life.

▦ The ideal size coffee table for a three-seat sofa is 30 inches wide by 41 inches deep by 17 inches high.

▦ It is better to have one or two items of quality than a room full of furniture and pictures: one great high piece and one favorite painting.

▦ Consider a touch of lacquer: black, bottle green, or Chinese red for a coffee table or an old box or a tray.

▦ Consider building a window ledge approximately 14 inches deep and 4 inches thick, directly under the windowframe. This ledge is the surface for flowers, magazines, and books.

▦ Clear Butcher's floor wax smells good and provides a nice shine for hardwood floors.

▦ To enhance your hardwood floors, small area rugs (4 by 6 feet) in front of the fireplace or sofa group add texture and color.

▦ In the summer, when you are not using your fireplace, place a decorative fire screen in front of it.

▦ Describe in your notebook how you want this room to feel and what colors you want to incorporate in the scheme.

▦ In keeping with a light, sunny feeling in the room, select clear, garden-fresh colors for your fabrics. All fabrics will soil and fade in time, but it's important to start out fresh.

▦ All colors that don't look well against pure white are muddy colors.

▩   Strike an equal balance between your upholstered pieces and your wood furniture. This will keep the room from becoming too "leggy."

▩   To avoid unnecessary clutter, group your collections by subject matter. Keep boxes together, silver together, enamel objects together; look for the common denominator.

▩   Consider mounting a favorite old decorative lacquer tray to use as a coffee table.

▩   As Mrs. Brown taught us: "Every room should have a touch of yellow."

▩   Windows are your connection with nature. Keep them clean at all times. All window trim should be painted semi-gloss (or gloss) enamel white to bring in more light.

▩   Window treatments should never cover the glass except at night for privacy.

▩   The floor is visibly one third of the room. A hardwood floor is ideal. Rip up old wall-to-wall carpeting to reveal the natural wood floors. Pry up a corner of any floor covering to see if there is wood underneath.

▩   Decide on the wood tones you like best for the room. Have the furniture and wood floor within the same color range. Dark mahogany furniture looks best on a dark brown floor, but pine pieces look best on a natural oak or pine floor.

▩   End tables do not have to match, but should be approximately the same height, from 26 to 30 inches. A 1-inch difference in height will not upset the balance.

▨ People like to put their feet up. Have a footstool approximately 1-inch lower in height than the chair.

▨ Sofas and chairs can be dressed up by pillows. You can add comfort as well as color by contrasting fabrics. To support the lower back, a 16- by 11-inch baby pillow is ideal. A large sofa can have two 23-inch-square pillows.

▨ You can display a small painting, as Mrs. Brown often did, by resting it on the back of the sofa, leaning against the wall.

▨ Put small pictures on easels. Use velvet or marbleized decorative paper to cover the ugly back of the frame. Remove any wire before gluing decorative fabric or paper to the back.

▨ This is one room to keep technology at bay. Try to position your stereo system so that it doesn't intrude on the room's aesthetics.

▨ When you place a loveseat adjacent to a wall, consider having a narrow table behind the loveseat to break up the bulk; it is an ideal place for flowers.

▨ Yes, family pictures belong in the living room. Group them together on a table.

▨ Dream about a favorite piece of furniture, and when you find it, don't worry where it will go. It will make the room and will be with you forever. Do you already have yours? I have a writing table that means the world to me.

▨ To create a simple country look, use white cotton tab café curtains hung from 1-inch wooden dowels, painted high-gloss enamel white.

▦ Remove all ceiling light fixtures and plaster the hole before painting the ceiling atmosphere blue. Decorative lamps are more attractive for this room.

▦ The living room is an ideal place to read. Consider building bookcases for your growing library. The back walls of the bookcases can be painted an accent color. Use Perfect Yellow, Fuller O'Brien 1-A-78.

▦ To determine how strong a color will look in your room, look at the inside of the paint can. The shadows inside the can act in much the same way as the walls of your room.

▦ Hang an old wooden display rack on the wall to show off your favorite porcelain. Include china fruits, vegetables, and dishes.

▦ Under the coffee table place a large basket brimming with potpourri and dried flowers.

▦ Place a favorite pair of candlesticks on the mantel; alternate different colors of beeswax candles—lettuce green, yellow, or pink.

▦ Always have a flower in a vase on your desk.

▦ Place your furniture for convenience and purpose. If you want to sit and read, place your chairs by the window with natural light and by the mantel for cozy evenings by the fire.

▦ Think of your living room as the most intimate and revealing room in your life. If you put your favorite things there, you will create an atmosphere that will be full of your spirit.

◫ Decide what the focal point of the room is, and build around that. If it is a mantel or a beautiful piece of furniture, you will be focusing inward. If you have an extraordinary view, the eye can extend beyond the limits of the walls.

◫ Think of the background of the space before you concern yourself with the contents. Get the bones right first.

◫ Select a background color that will enable you to change fabrics and decorations.

◫ Buy a pint of each paint color and put up several different samples. Look at the color in daylight and at night. Scotch-tape white paper all around the new sample so your eye can see it alone.

◫ If you have a wood floor, put it in good condition. Wall-to-wall carpeting is a substitute for a wood floor.

◫ Check the swing of each door. Decide whether you want doors or just an opening without doors.

◫ If there is a door leading to another room that you don't want to use, consider sheet-rocking the wall and eliminating the door and frame.

◫ If a picture molding hangs down the wall and it is not connected to the cornice molding at the ceiling, eliminate it unless you intend to hang art from it.

◫ If you have applied moldings on your plaster walls that break up the wall space and limit your ability to hang art, remove them.

▦ Strip your windows of all curtains, valances, and shades. Study your windows bare. Evaluate their style and proportion as well as the quality of light you gain.

▦ The better the view, the less need for a fancy window treatment. Look at a bare window as you would at someone with no makeup or hairstyle.

▦ Think of your view throughout the changing seasons.

▦ If you require air conditioning, consider having a unit put in the wall under the window so you can benefit from all your light and view.

▦ If you have a radiator that has a cover built over it, remove the cover and examine the heating unit. Chances are you can replace it with a smaller, more efficient radiator.

▦ Check to be sure you have enough electrical outlets. Most living rooms are too dark.

▦ If you are an art collector and like lights attached to your picture frames, consider putting in gem boxes in the center of each wall 60 inches from the floor to the center of the box to avoid cords hanging down the walls.

▦ If you have a fireplace that is not operative, consider eliminating it. A focal point should not be artificial.

▦ The mantel's design, scale, material, and color will be main features in the room. If you inherit a room with a hideous black and orange marble mantel that ruins the space, consider painting the mantel white to match the woodwork.

▓ If your room is paneled in a knotty orange pine, feel free to paint over the wood. A delicious peach or yellow color may suit you better.

▓ If your wood floors are dark and hard to maintain, sand and scrape them and stain them a warm, fruitwood color.

▓ If the ceiling is low, have a strong contrast in the tone of the floor. A rule of thumb is for the floor to be a darker color than the walls, which will make the room more grounded.

▓ Get to know and understand the pure space, day and night, before you fill it up.

▓ Decide how you want to use this room seven days a week, not for occasional guests and parties.

▓ Place a chair or sofa where you would like to sit when alone in the room.

▓ Place another sofa or a few chairs where you would like to sit and have an intimate conversation.

▓ If your room is small, fewer pieces of normal-sized uphol-stered furniture will look better than crowding the space with smaller-scaled furnishings.

▓ Always keep the human scale in mind when selecting furni-ture. A chair never has to be enormous; it has to envelop and support a man or woman.

▓ If your room is large, select normal-scaled furniture and make several distinctly different seating arrangements.

🔳 Repeat shapes. Have pairs of four matching chairs. Mrs. Brown taught us that repetition brings harmony.

🔳 Decide on the style you are trying to achieve. This will help you edit out things that don't apply.

🔳 Commit yourself to one favorite piece of furniture and build around it.

🔳 When you order upholstered chairs, have them put on swivels. It is liberating to be able to swing around to watch a sunset or to sit by a warm fire.

🔳 For each chair or sofa, there should be a table to put a book or drink.

🔳 You should be able to read in all the seating areas in your living room. Have lamps on dimmer switches and install three-way switches for flexible lighting.

🔳 One large coffee table will anchor the room. It should serve people at a sofa and surrounding chairs.

🔳 Hang pictures so they are at eye level when people are standing. Sixty inches to the center of the picture is a good rule of thumb.

🔳 If you don't have a lot of wall decorations and the floor is bare, select one fabric and use it on all your furniture to give the room impact.

🔳 If your furniture designs aren't ideal in style or scale, choose a patterned fabric and blend them together.

🔳 If you have well-proportioned upholstery, woven colorful textiles can create a harmonious, serene feeling.

▦ Look at furniture from all angles. Often, we see furniture from the back or sides. You may want to "float" a sofa in the middle of the room.

▦ Glass coffee tables are dangerous, especially when there are small children around.

▦ The design of a printed fabric should be an attractive scale when you are seeing it close up.

▦ Use chintz or a printed fabric, generously so that it doesn't look sparse.

▦ Move your tabletop accessories around. Never dust a table without rearranging your treasures. You will enjoy them more when you see them fresh.

▦ Move your art every few months.

▦ If you feel you need curtains, extend them approximately 8 inches out on each side of the window wall so you won't block out any light.

▦ If your windows are low, you can install bamboo shades or valances above their openings to raise the appearance of the windows.

▦ Indoor shutters give the illusion of a garden beyond, and they control light well.

▦ If you have indoor shutters, consider having a window ledge extend the width of the shutters so that when they are open, they appear to be supported architecturally.

▓ Invest in one beautiful painting or mirror as a focal point in the room.

▓ Let the colors of your living room represent the color scheme for your whole house.

▓ Get your color inspirations from nature. If you love flowers in your garden, bring them into your room by using flowered chintz, botanical floral prints, and a flowered needlepoint rug.

▓ Put a colorful silk tassel on a key that is inserted in a drawer of a cabinet.

▓ Use one color fabric on the front of a knife-edge pillow and another color on the back. Use decorative silk cord in the seam to make the pillow reversible.

▓ Hide a bolt of leftover fabric under the sofa concealed by the flounce so you can re-cover a cushion or patch a worn chair arm as needed.

▓ Start collecting things — ribbons, boxes, swatches, anything — in the colors you love. These odds and ends become your palette.

▓ Use mirrors architecturally to fool the eye and enlarge the space. Hang a mirror between two windows to make it appear as one large opening.

▓ If you have a working fireplace, group some upholstered chairs, a loveseat, or a sofa around the hearth for the winter months.

▓ Place a stack of favorite picture books on coffee and end tables.

▣ Place a plant in a copper or brass bucket to reflect more light.

▣ Use your favorite colors everywhere. Let the living room show off the entire rainbow; then play up or play down its various hues elsewhere.

▣ Be consistent with the treatment of all four walls in the room.

▣ Stain the wood floors the same shade in all public areas.

▣ Paint the trim semi-gloss white, not just in the living room, but in every room in the house, because it frames each room and helps to unify the whole house.

Chapter 7

DINING PLACES

Next to the living room, the dining room is the least understood and appreciated room in the house. The pace
and clutter of our long, tightly scheduled days draw us away
from the full satisfaction we should derive from the important
daily ritual of dining with loved ones. There is nothing more
beautiful than people sitting around the table in an alchemy of
spirit and companionship. Good food is pleasing, but the reality
is that when we sit down with family and friends for a meal, food
is not the most important element, nor is the physical space. The
key to wonderful dining is the chemistry of the company. In the
right frame of mind, we are more receptive to all the sensual
pleasures that a meal provides.

Our dining spaces can help create this essential attitude and
ambience. When we are authentic, when we keep our spaces
simple, simply beautiful living takes place. Food is extremely important to me, as it was to my favorite artist, Claude Monet, who
loved to eat and was quite particular about his mealtime rituals.
I'm certain it was a spur to him, as he painted through the morning (he often rose before dawn), to know that at precisely 11:30
A.M., lunch would be served to him and his guests in his airy
cream and daffodil-yellow dining room in Giverny. Meals were

*Timeless classic
elegance*

123

served on blue and white porcelain china inspired by the Japanese. He had a hugh appetite for life, food, conversation, and drink; and he had the vision to know how to live beautifully.

It would be many years before I had my own dining room. As a young wife and mother, I had created a series of impromptu spaces, beginning with the dining table constructed out of an old door placed over two sawhorses and covered with a finished fabric remnant. I used pinking shears to balloon the skirt to brush against our highly polished bare wood floor. This was living! Later, when we moved to another apartment, we made a country dining room out of an unneeded maid's room. We called it "The Cave" because its white, rough plaster walls and terracotta floor reminded us of a French wine cellar. The plywood banquette we made was covered with a soft, comfortable cushion, and the back was lined with lively patterned cotton pillows.

When Peter and I married, I moved to his apartment, where he had raised six children. Again, the dream of having a proper dining room eluded me. But after eighteen years of marriage, the large French provincial table that lives in our foyer (and that doubles as my work area) suits me just fine. We have hosted many memorable lunch and dinner parties in that charming space. Size, and traditional room labels, mean little. With the right table settings, with candles and fresh flowers perfuming the air, any space, no matter how humble, can become enchanted.

As you begin to contemplate your dining area, think about the importance of the mealtime rituals in your life. Do you prefer a formal or informal dining room setting? When you plan meals and special menus, do you think about how the food will look on the table? Do you like to entertain? Do you prefer large or intimate parties? What is the daily traffic flow through your dining room? The answers to these and other questions will help inform your furniture choices and placement, and overall decorating scheme.

For instance, when I finally got that longed-for dining room in our Stonington house, I was immediately charmed by the

I discovered true English-country style during a trip to England.
—Mario Buatta

room, which was huge and had an angled fireplace and windows on two walls. But the room also had doors—lots of them: a side door to the house; a door to the basement; and openings to the living room, staircase, kitchen, and back hall, as well as a linen storage closet! So the first thing we did was to remove four doors to bring in more light and let the room breathe.

Examine your walls and determine what will work best for your space. You may decide to close *up* a door opening in order to put a long sideboard against a solid wall, or to break open a wall to join the dining room with part of the kitchen. If you don't wish to marry two rooms completely, possibly an arched opening would be successful, with arched doors you can close when you want privacy. If you need all the doors, but don't want your space to look like a gallery of openings, consider having a concealed door instead. This is done with Joss hinges and looks like part of the wall when closed.

The way you decide to use your dining space will guide your color scheme as well as your other decisions. For instance, if your living room flows into the dining area, or is separated from it by a center hall (as in the style of many Colonial houses), color and flooring choices need not precisely match, but should be complementary in order to tie the spaces together.

Dining rooms, like bedrooms, were traditionally the rooms most likely to introduce wallpaper into the house. Now, instead, I suggest covering the walls more simply so they won't be limited or compete with the colors and textures of table arrangements, eating accessories, and the decorative objects on the walls and surface areas. An all green and white room comes alive when you use pink napkins and lily-of-the-valley plates and have pink hyacinths sitting in clay pots. While your overall color scheme may be carried down to the dishware, mats, and other linens, don't agonize about having all the colors match up completely, or worry that your wedding china will clash or appear cluttered and confusing. Good service plates will tie the room's look together before everyone sits down. When you begin to eat, and

The dining table is the last retreat of the old values and more human scale of the past.
— Patrick Dunne

as successive courses are served, no one will be looking at the walls much. They will be looking at their plates and at each other!

Try not to limit yourself to using the same tablecloth at every meal. You can set the mood and tone of an evening meal by your selection of plates, napkins, and glassware. The fun part is arranging accessories so that they have special meaning and all fit well together. Your objects will add interest to the room—while your wall covering and fabric choices will provide background for them.

Dining in a strongly colored room can be elegant. White trim in a dark room keeps it from being gloomy, is a welcome contrast, and sets off the walls beautifully. The strong wall color gives a background for your wood furniture, for a carpet or area rug, and creates a cozy feeling. But when selecting your dining room color, make sure it comes alive in candlelight. Test your paint sample at home in candlelight before you commit to it. No lighting choice—whether it be a chandelier, recessed lights with dimmer switches, sconces, or table or standing lamps—bathes a room in intimacy the way candlelight does.

Home can be a visceral experience.

When clients begin to make dining room furniture choices, I invariably tell them to start with the table. I've always enjoyed dining at round tables at friends' houses. There's something so gracious about being in a circle. Conversation can be more general than when sitting at a rectangular table. But we all have space restrictions and so it's also important to keep your selections flexible. When you are free to move and arrange your furniture so that it works for six, eight, or fifty, you'll find your life is so simplified. While a 72-inch-round glass tabletop may accentuate the gorgeous colors of your dhurrie area rug, or a sensuous granite slab on dramatic marble pedestals give your space and ultra-modern look, these surfaces weigh a ton and will limit you as you move from one situation to another. Your room has to have furniture that adapts.

If you already have furniture you wish to use — for example, a charming American country hutch — or need to work around built-ins such as windowseats or corner cupboards, they will naturally dictate your other choices. Place the furniture you have so that it fits in to the best advantage and work from there. I know a woman who entertains frequently and favors large sit-down dinners where guests help themselves. Her French provincial–inspired dining room features a carved, mahogany buffet and a long country-style tiled shelf for hot dishes. The serving shelf rescues the room from appearing heavy and overcomplicated by too much wood, while the walls remain visible above and below the shelf.

As I have cautioned elsewhere, try to stay away from matched dining room sets. Feel free to blend your wooden pieces. Your chairs should be lightweight, graceful, and easily carried from room to room. For larger parties, you can supplement the dining room chairs with others of complementary size and proportion from your living room. Nothing, however, looks more stiff than a dining room cluttered up with too many extra chairs of the same design. If you're lucky enough to have a table that expands to seat twelve, and there are twelve matching chairs along the walls, dancing class–style, store them elsewhere — or better yet, move them into other rooms where they, too, may be enjoyed daily.

We adore our Connecticut dining room so much that we have seized on it as a space for everyday living. Initially, we pulled our French farm table up close to the fireplace and used it as a partner's desk where we worked on correspondence and did our writing. We loved facing the fire and had a huge woodpile stacked at handy reach so we could stay comfortably warm as we worked during the cold country winters. The fact that we didn't actually use this room at first for entertaining in no way diminished its meaning and benefit to us. On the contrary, we ate our meals by the warm fire and drank hot broth there in the

Whatever pleases—
just whatever
pleases.
—Janet McCaffery

afternoons. While we were renovating the house we probably spent more quality time as a couple in our dining room than we would have if it had immediately been a dining room, lingering over a cup of coffee, reading the Sunday paper, doing a puzzle, enjoying a good conversation.

So when the time came to get down to business to create my first real dining room, I tried to keep this space adaptable to these many uses. As much as any of us may love to entertain, our dining rooms are only another manifestation of the real living that goes on at home.

We began by moving the country table away from the fireplace to the center of the room. Around it we arranged six Windsor side chairs; we placed a country Queen Anne chair at one end, and at the other, a rustic armchair we found in Bermuda. I love old chairs, and scattered around are children's chairs (both Windsor and ladderback), so that visiting small ones can easily snuggle into the group. Vertical focal points become important in dining areas, given the low rectangularity of your principal furniture. In our case, we used two high pine cupboards and installed shelf lighting to show off our colorful dishes and porcelain objects.

It was an unexpected blessing that our dining room had a closet for tablecloths and napkins. For once, I can see everything at a glance (in New York the napkins are in a chest of drawers and the tablecloths are in a hall linen closet, so it's difficult to coordinate the two when I set the table). In Connecticut I've made different sets of flowered cloths and complementary napkins and tied them all up in neat ribbons, ready to go. At a glance I can see how many napkins there are. I love variety, and I often leave the table bare wood and just use colorful napkins. My table dressing impulses have a lot to do with the weather. If it's rainy and dark out, I'm tempted to cover the brown wood table with a bright flowered cotton cloth to add cheer. I enjoy lively table coverings in the winter, too. If you're similarly inclined to vary

There is nothing more trite than a set period.
—Eleanor McMillen Brown

your table decor, this is another way to underscore the value of keeping wall treatments simple and unfussy.

While Peter and I seldom move our table to the fire anymore, we have come to understand that a dining room's major message is that of life lived between these four walls. Hospitality truly does begin at home. The more you *alone* can use and enjoy this room, the more pleasure you will bring to any others you ask to join you there. It really doesn't matter in the end how many chairs you have. You can always pull up an extra one, even if it's a folding chair. It doesn't matter how many people you can seat; you can always move things around and set up a card table. We all want to feel welcome. We all want to break bread among ourselves and enjoy each other's company in an attractive setting. So light a few candles, make a toast, and celebrate together.

GRACE NOTES

▩ Ideally, have a table that seats eight. This is the best number for people to be able to communicate and celebrate together. You can always add folding tables for larger groups.

▩ Use this space throughout the day as well as evenings. The table is one of the most useful surfaces in your home.

▩ Your room decoration needn't be any more formal than the rest of your home. When a room becomes overdone, it becomes pretentious. A butcher block table can always be dressed up with a pretty tablecloth.

▩ Recall your favorite restaurant. Besides the good food, what was it about the ambience that spoke to you that you can re-create at home?

▓ Every day can be a memorable celebration. Use your favorite dishes, napkins, and accessories to brighten up daily mealtimes.

▓ Don't hide your beautiful dishes. A high pine or walnut cabinet can show off your favorite porcelain treasures.

▓ If there's room for it, have another long table you can use as a serving area for festive meals.

▓ You can never have enough candles in the dining room.

▓ To break up the brown tones of the floor, table, and chairs, you may want a flat wool dhurrie rug that adds color and pattern. Bring a few of your favorite dishes for inspiration when you go to select a rug.

▓ Always have something fresh and natural as a centerpiece on the dining room table: lemons, limes, oranges, red and green apples, grapes, and pears.

▓ To add color and comfort, select a small-scaled dress fabric and make knife-edge (two seams sewn together without a border) cushions for each chair, using ribbons to tie them to the back legs.

▓ Don't hide the beauty of your wood table under fancy tablecloths except on special occasions.

▓ Your table should be 11 to 13 inches higher than the chair-seat height. If you or your spouse are tall, be sure the apron (the wood panel under the tabletop) isn't too deep because you want to be able to cross your legs.

▦ Run your fingers under the apron and with the fine side of an emery board, sand until smooth any rough spots. There's nothing more irritating than snagging stockings or trousers when you cross your legs.

▦ When you want to mix different chairs, be sure that the seat heights are compatible, the scale is similar, and they are of the same general style.

▦ If you have a young child, hunt around antiques fairs for an old wooden high chair. Long after the child is grown and has left home, you'll keep the attractive high chair in the dining area as a warm memory and for future generations.

▦ To determine whether to wallpaper or paint this space, consider how many wall hangings you have. If you can decorate the walls with prints, paintings, mirrors, quilts, or porcelain plates, paint is a better choice, or a simple striped wallpaper.

▦ If your dining room has little natural light, you can lighten the tone of the wood floor to give a cheerier appearance. Stain the saddle (the raised wooden strip in a doorway) the color of the adjacent room.

▦ Keep your window treatment light and understated so the room is relaxed and cheerful during the day. A cloud shade of soft pretty, pastel plaid could be ideal.

▦ If your room has a country flavor, use a simple stencil to create interest under the cornice molding. Even by itself, a stencil will add height and interest to the room.

▦ If your floors are in bad condition, consider sanding them and staining them with a rich green or French blue aniline. If the room is not irregular in shape, you can hand-paint a floral border on the floor or use a simple stencil pattern.

▓ Inspired by Claude Monet's dining room at Giverny, paint your old dining table butter yellow. Create a color scheme of shades of blue, yellow, and white.

▓ Your beautiful silver will add elegance to any meal. We have an inherited silver pitcher, which we use every day for ice water. When setting the table, use different colored napkins and a variety of favorite flowered plates.

▓ Consider all the ways you like to entertain. Locate the possible eating places in your house or apartment, inside and out-of-doors. Determine what styles and circumstances are most compatible at each spot, as well as how many people you can serve at each location.

▓ Yellow walls make dark woods look elegant. Perfect Yellow, Fuller O'Brien, 1-A-78, is lively with white trim and dark wood furniture.

▓ White plates show off food beautifully, like an artist's blank canvas. Think of the food you serve as a work of art.

Chapter 8

KITCHENS

$\mathcal{I}$n every house there is bound to be a room or space that is so dreadful that you close your eyes and shut the door until you have the strength to face it. Our horror was our kitchen — particularly the buttery, or butler's pantry — on the north side of the house. This room was dark, with peeling paint, a raised linoleum floor (indicating multiple layers of former floor coverings), and so filled with heavy cupboard doors as to make it feel cagelike. The windowpanes in the kitchen had been painted over, the window frames painted shut. The task of lifting the room from its depression seemed formidable but to be practical, we had to get down to it quickly, as kitchens are the hub and heartbeat of family life.

Long before we fell in love with our dear cottage, previous owners had installed a white Formica island in the middle of this wasteland, a decision that was clearly out of place in this old, quaint house. "Out of here!" we exclaimed at once, and doing so immediately improved the space. Most of us mistakenly assume that when we see something structural in a room that it belongs or must remain. And thus we compound someone else's decorating mistakes by trying — usually futilely — to build around

Just do an excellent job and the money will follow.
—Eleanor McMillen Brown

them or throw money at them in some ill-advised solution. As much as I like the islands and peninsulas that are popular in contemporary kitchens, it was a joy to eliminate that awkward, bulky island. And once the correct scale and proportion of the room reemerged, the kitchen began to speak to us as a place we could make beautiful and be drawn to.

I began with simple things so that I could feel encouraged by immediate results. I banged open the windows and had clean glass installed, and was instantly cheered by the sight of geraniums peeking into the kitchen from the window box outside. Along with two hard-working women we hired to assist us, we tore off the cupboard doors to expose the plain shelves, banged open the drawers, also painted over, and removed the fake ornamental hardware.

The peeling paint in the pantry came down in huge clumps, revealing layers and layers of flowered wallpaper and at least a dozen ugly paint colors. We sanded and spackled the walls, and began to paint them a high-gloss white to open them up to the light. We selected a deep purple-blue (Velvet Morning) for the kitchen trim and for the backs of the pantry shelves, and slowly these two rooms started to come together.

The floor, however, was a nagging problem. After the linoleum was removed, our contractor advised us that the only way to take off the thick layer of sticky tar and gummy glue underneath would be by hand. So we set to work with hammers and chisels. But after three grueling all-morning sessions of this, we had only a postage-stamp–size section of wood to show for our efforts. It appeared as though our mission could not be accomplished.

I was alone in the house the following week. With Peter away at a business conference, I was free to work from dawn to midnight without a critical warning that it was time to stop and go to bed. The exterior renovation of the house was reaching a crescendo with the installation of a new front door and other refinements, and I was feeling invigorated. I edged more cupboard

The homeliest tasks get beautiful if loving hands do them.
—Louisa May Alcott

shelves in Velvet Morning and put another coat of white and blue paint on the respective pantry and kitchen walls. I caulked the cracks on the window ledges; I painted the new, inexpensive wood drawer pulls we'd purchased blue, to contrast with the white drawers. I stripped and painted the kitchen door and moldings, and had Jim, our contractor, rehinge the door so that it would swing the other way to open up the kitchen area better. But I cringed each time my eye went to that tar floor.

Finally, I went to Jim and begged him to please find a way of getting through that layer of tar and glue to the original floor underneath. I explained that I was willing to face the possibility that it could be entirely rotten, and that I'd have to assume the expense of replacing it. Well, all things are sweetened by risk. Jim set to work with a crowbar and heavy-duty hammer and slowly pried up the tar-drenched floor to reveal the beautiful original pine wood underneath. Fortunately, only one floorboard required replacing; we removed the gummy saddle so the floorboards between the kitchen and pantry flowed in an unbroken line. After sanding the floor and vacuuming the surface dust, I took a breather—and studied the results.

I observed that the floorboards were laid vertically as you entered the room. In a narrow space, like our pantry, it is always best to try to expand the dimension vertically. To make the room look bigger, I painted alternating planks in blue and white stripes. Today, this once monstrous area has become the focal point of the back of our house!

The transformation of our pantry was a breakthrough for us. We were now able to decorate the kitchen, to claim it as the heart of our domestic life. We started by upgrading the appliances, and then we placed our round French farm table in the center of the room. We put lightly painted folding garden chairs with wooden seats around the table, placed some flowers in a faïence soup tureen on it, and the room began to sing.

*Cultivate the habit
of attention.*

❖

One of our favorite paintings is a Roger Mŭhl still life of an al fresco luncheon party. Half-filled glasses of red wine, plates of ripened fruits and cheeses, and bread crumbs on the table are witnesses to a pleasant meal. The picture takes up the entire wall space above an old-fashioned muffin warmer and gives us the feeling of laughter and happiness shared. Why did I hang a good oil painting in the kitchen? Because I know that a little soap and water can clean it if it becomes dirty. If we spend a lot of time in a place, we shouldn't be afraid to bring in the things we love to enjoy and look at! Against an adjacent wall we placed a large nineteenth-century butcher block table, and over it we hung a pine plate rack to display some of our favorite Italian pottery.

This room has come alive. Instead of using the kitchen only for food preparation and for meals, we now love to sit there and talk. In fact, until you do spend relaxed time in a room, you won't understand its potential. One evening after we'd been for dinner at a friend's house, I asked Peter if he wanted to stop by a café near our house for a nightcap. Peter said, "What a great idea, but let's go home instead to our own café." That evening, as we sat bathed in candlelight sipping Chardonnay at the kitchen table, we were awakened to a whole new place to be together, to talk and listen, or be silent. We are drawn to places where we envision we may find serenity or stimulation, but always with the idea that it will make us feel good to be there. We don't choose to spend time in a place that will lower our spirits. Often, as with our kitchen, a room needs an enormous amount of work before you can start to build in the ambience you desire.

When you begin to address your own kitchen design, you must determine whether the look you want to create is country and casual, or sophisticated, minimalist, and contemporary. This is the most important decision you will make about the kitchen because cabinetry is your biggest ticket item and once you've committed yourself, you cannot change it.

Unlike the furniture in other rooms, kitchen furniture—cab-

To be of use in the world is the only way to be happy.
—Eleanor McMillen Brown

inets, countertops, and appliances—cannot be moved about in trial-and-error fashion. So draw a floor plan, paying special attention to convenience and practicality. You don't want the stove to be too far away from the sink, and you don't want to cross the room in order to get into the refrigerator!

Also, as you plan your space, ask yourself if the kitchen is a room where you enjoy spending a lot of time. Do you eat most of your meals there? Is it well organized and are you? Do you prefer to stow everything behind cupboard doors in order to keep your work surfaces clear, or do you like having your kitchen implements handy and within easy reach? How much storage space do you require? Have you remembered to factor your recycling needs into this space? What kind of appliances do you prefer; single or double ovens; a built-in microwave or one that sits on the countertop; single or side-by-side refrigerator/freezers? What work and floor surface materials do you like? Wood? Tile? Butcher block? Formica? Corian? The choices are many and dizzying, so do not hesitate to look at magazines to see what's available. Do your homework by visiting kitchen appliance stores. These crucial decisions will affect the layout and design of your space.

Kitchens are busy-looking by nature, and the walls are usually broken up into odd shapes. For this reason I suggest you keep the wall treatment simple. You can either paint them a high-gloss enamel so they are scrubbable, or you can hang a paper- or canvas-backed vinyl. Rough plaster walls in a kitchen are nice because they create a romantic atmosphere; but if you favor patterned wallpaper, pick one with a small repeat so it can be cut up but still retain the intended impact. If you go this route, be sure to keep your ceilings and trim light.

Because kitchen cabinets count for a large part of your total wall area, their style and color should be tied together with your walls and/or woodwork. You can accomplish this by contrasting colors dramatically or by having them closely related. For ex-

Everything is an autobiography.

ample: Dark wood cabinets look beautiful against white walls. No matter what you do, your cabinets should be beautiful and cleanable. Wood is popular for just this reason. Friends in California blended stainless steel refrigerator/freezer covers, granite countertops, and bird's-eye maple cabinetry, leavening the commercial, industrial look with this warm and inviting wood. Or you can refreshen your current wood cabinets by painting or treating them in an exciting way. Formica can be ordered in just about any color you wish, or your old cabinets can be given a face-lift by simply installing new decorative doors. Finally, if you have glass-fronted cabinets, think twice before replacing them. There is no more charming way to display your prettiest crystal, glass, and china. They'll add depth, sparkle, and color to the room. Hang Mylar silver-foil paper on the backs of your cupboards for an added dimension; art supply stores sell it by the yard, sticky-backed.

After your cabinets are planned, you must turn next to your refrigerator, sink, dishwasher, and stove. These necessary pieces of equipment have to have a relationship to the other elements because they dominate your space and therefore must go together. Appliance manufacturers will cut dishwasher, oven, and refrigerator door panels to your size specifications. Your sink can be porcelain (which is made in a wide variety of colors) or stainless steel; but I strongly advise you not to order a double sink unless each is big enough for cleaning large cookware.

Your floors provide a wonderful way to bring beauty and atmosphere into a potentially sterile area, and here I always think it's best to use a natural material, if possible. Wood is very easy to maintain. I'm a big advocate of cork, which is inexpensive and feels comfortable under your feet. Brick, stone, ceramic, or quarry tiles are more costly but can create your whole kitchen atmosphere. Look into the expense and study your options carefully. There are many attractive vinyl floor products on the mar-

The estimate is the job.
—Eleanor McMillen Brown

ket today. But whatever you decide to use, remember to relate your flooring choice to your other kitchen plans and schemes.

Decorative glazed tiles are wonderful if you are willing to splurge on them, particularly behind your counters. These walls are central to the total kitchen design, and so they will be fully appreciated. When measuring, allow space for grouting in between each tile. Small-sized tiles will actually make your space look larger; large tiles contract the space. If you can't afford to tile right away, paint the back of your counter walls until you have the funds, or purchase just a few hand-painted tiles and intersperse them in an attractive design with plainer ones.

Kitchens can be terribly dark on gray days, so lighting is a very important element to incorporate into your overall design. Be sure your work stations (stove, sink, and countertops) are properly lighted, and control your impulse to use fluorescent ceiling lights, however practical they are for general illumination. Instead, your counters can be lighted from underneath the raised cabinets, or you can experiment with track lighting. Remember, too, that lighting must come on very strong and also disappear instantly. For cooking, you need to see; for serving and dining, you need mood lighting.

Color, of course, will pull all these disparate choices together. But the fewer colors you use in your kitchen, the more outstanding the effect can be; and the fewer drastic color changes in the room, the better. For strength, start at the ground by using an earthy floor tone, which is practical for hiding dirt; then go up to a lighter-colored bottom cabinet, countertop, and upper cabinet; and finish with light walls. Most of us tend to go with light kitchen walls, since kitchens are often such dark rooms.

Because kitchens have few portable pieces of furniture, select your tables and chairs and whatever else you can comfortably accommodate thoughtfully, with an eye toward comfort as well as aesthetics. Banquettes can be installed by your carpenter at modest cost, covered with pretty fabrics and cushioned by dec-

My heart has finally found a home.
—Mary Ann Petro

orative throw pillows. Friends in Portland, Oregon, created a casual country look for their table by selecting old wicker chairs they picked up at auction, repainting them in soft, pastel colors, and cushioning them in prefaded cotton fabric with zippered covers for easy laundering. Generally, however, I don't believe in fabrics in kitchens. They get dirty too quickly. When my girls were small, we covered a banquette cushion in our second New York apartment in a natural linen and it looked marvelous. For one week! We recovered it in a patent-leather vinyl and it still looked fabulous—but we could sponge it clean after each meal. Wood is a good choice for this same reason. A client found a delightful set of chairs hand-painted with farm animals, which looks splendid with her long pine kitchen table. The chairs were originally of unfinished wood, purchased from a stock supplier; they were acrylic-painted and protected by several coats of sturdy polyurethane. (If you're artistically inclined, you can easily create your own seating designs!)

If space allows, I also think it's wonderful to invest in one important display piece to bring color, texture, or fancy into the room. Some clients selected traditional white glass-fronted cabinetry, dark marble countertops, and a black-and-white checked tile floor. They also purchased a charming bread warmer, an old-fashioned country piece still in its original red paint, to add some zip and whimsy to the room. A friend uses a large antique hutch that extends across the length of one wall to display her plates and glassware; while another friend uses a delicate, glass-shelved baker's rack on which to display plants and other decorative ornaments.

While even the most traditional among us have succumbed to certain kitchen gadgets and gimmickry in the last years, I see no reason why we cannot be nourished by beautifully designed equipment throughout our kitchen spaces. Take inventory of your cookware, spice rack, clock, and teakettle. These are items you use every day and so you deserve to have them be attractive.

Lately I have been thinking how comfort is perhaps the ultimate luxury.
—Billy Baldwin

The cool efficiency of the Cuisinart, blender, and electric can opener can be balanced by pretty mixing bowls and crockery. Cookbooks, some tomatoes ripening on the windowsill, will soften and individualize any kitchen.

Bring your personal treasures into your kitchen and create decorative appointments. These may be as simple as a collection of framed restaurant menus to remind you of memorable meals or a nest of baskets stacked nonchalantly in the corner. I know a woman who created a framed wall collage out of her son's summer camp art projects: A watermelon slice made from colored construction paper; a flat, lattice "sculpture" made from popsicle sticks; gold Mylar fish; a watercolor sailboat; a puppy dog with felt ears and nose made from a simple brown lunchbag surround her son's sweet camp photograph. It hangs on a wall near her center island, where she can catch glimpses of it while preparing meals.

I turned that buttery we so successfully assaulted into a charming area for displaying colorful pottery and porcelain. After living in cramped apartments for most of my adult life, it gave me great pleasure finally to bring my favorite objects out into the open. Peter and I spent a memorable Saturday afternoon working together to put these things in their places. We hung plates, rested dishes on racks, placed the pitchers and dinnerware we had gathered at different periods of our marriage and during wonderful trips taken with the children. As we experimented with various groupings, arranging them with respect to their form, size, color, and scale, each piece became an occasion to take a sentimental journey, and the finished buttery a shrine to memories we can live each day.

We can transform the darkest, nastiest corners of our house into dream places. Peter never wanted to spend time in our kitchen until this transformation. Now we retreat into this magical room to sip a cool drink, to putter, arrange flowers, open mail, talk on the telephone. In our kitchen, we feel the good life

Balance

and we are living it fully right here. In our kitchen, we have found a way of turning a repetitious act like making the morning coffee into a meditation.

Like the rest of your house, the kitchen should be a place that feeds you emotionally. The reason so many of us enjoy eating here is because the atmosphere is homey, unpretentious, and constant. I do believe that the pendulum is swinging back to simplicity in our kitchen designs. No matter how modern or convenient, efficient, and well designed, the kitchen is the place where we pass on to our children many of our domestic patterns. So many important lessons are taught by example here. If the memories of conviviality and spirit are good ones, our children will never fully leave home. They will visit often to replenish themselves from that well of harmony and contentment that sustains us all.

GRACE NOTES

▦ Because the kitchen is the heart of every home, make it the warmest room in your life. Use as many organic materials as possible, such as wood, tiles, cork, plaster, baskets, terra-cotta.

▦ Thirty-seven inches is an ideal counter height for most people. If you are over 6 feet 2 inches tall, perhaps you should have at least one countertop that is 41 to 43 inches high so you will be comfortable when standing.

▦ The ideal height difference between counter and stool is 11 inches. For example, the 41-inch-high counter height can also accommodate a 30-inch-high stool, which you can use when telephoning or preparing food.

▦ If you are planning new countertops, consider installing a 1¾-inch-thick butcher block. If the block is of unsealed maple, you can scrub it clean with hot water and a Brillo pad. To eliminate stains, use a sanding block and some Ajax or Comet cleanser.

▨ Upper cabinets should be placed 14 to 15 inches above the countertops.

▨ Counters should vary in depth from 22 to 28 inches.

▨ If you intend to use high stools at a counter island or peninsula, the overhang should measure between 10 and 12 inches.

▨ Install strip lighting under the upper cabinets using 2-inch GE Cool Bright clear light bulbs; only 5 watts, and that can be moved in sockets to add more light where needed.

▨ Install 6-foot ceiling tracks can lighting fixtures that use Parr reflector bulbs. Aim these cans down at the stove, sink, kitchen table, and counters. An average kitchen requires at least 500 watts of light when food is being prepared.

▨ Install Ipocork, 12-inch squares of vinyl laminated cork, on the floor for sound absorption, foot comfort, and a clean, simple, natural, Swedish look. These tiles are easy to cut and install yourself.

▨ Paint wooden kitchen floorboards in alternating colors, using white for one of them as a visual anchor. Paint the cabinets and walls white and the trim in the semi-gloss of a contrasting color.

▨ Place a colorful rag rug in front of the kitchen sink.

■ To create a feeling of the south of France, rough-plaster your walls. Get instructions from your local paint store.

■ Build an 8- to 12-inch window ledge for your herbs and plants. Use 4-inch decorative tiles to cover the surface of the ledge.

■ Hang shiny copper pots on the wall to reflect light and for decoration.

■ Have your appliances spray-painted the same color as the cabinets. Give a sample of the cabinet color to the appliance manufacturer, which will make the paint so that it adheres to the metal appliances.

■ Install old-fashioned brass and porcelain hot and cold fixtures for your sink.

■ The warmest kitchens always have a free-standing table. If you can find an old one, it will add charm and character.

■ Hang a collection of baskets on 1½-inch brads (nails without heads). Use the baskets for bread, fruit, and flowering plants.

■ Install a rack with individual compartments for wines, mineral water, and soda bottles measuring approximately 5 inches long by 4¼ inches wide by 11 inches deep. Not only is the rack good for storing bottles, it is also extremely decorative.

■ Hang a collection of favorite pottery dishes on wall-mounted spring plate racks to brighten up a blank wall. Place three to five in a grouping.

■ Replace your old, worn-out stainless steel sink with an in-expensive over-counter white porcelain sink approximately 16 by 22 by 8 inches.

■ Install in the sink a high goosenecked faucet approximately 14 to 17 inches long so you can clean roasting pans and tall flower vases.

■ Paint all trim and cabinets inside and out high-gloss Blue Charm Fuller O'Brien 1-D-44. The soothing sky color will refresh your spirits as you work in your kitchen.

■ Have a small basket next to your sink filled with a variety of colorful scented soaps.

■ Hang an unusual, large, fun clock that keeps good time on a prominent wall.

■ Buy a 10-foot-long telephone extension cord so you can move freely around your kitchen and be productive as you talk on the telephone.

■ Consider having one counter-tiled with blue and white tiles to remind you of Claude Monet's kitchen in Giverny.

■ Install decorative tiles on the walls between the countertops and the bottoms of the cabinets. Country Floors, Inc., New York City, imports decorative tiles from all over Europe.

■ Store a collection of clean glass pitchers on top of the refrigerator.

■ Always keep a cup of sharp pencils, a notepad, scissors, and a memo board for messages next to the telephone.

◪ Store your best silver in a kitchen drawer lined with Pacific cloth. Have a locksmith install a lock, for safety.

◪ Use large glass decanters to store your oil and vinegar near the stove.

◪ Try to keep counter spaces clear for spontaneous projects — pasting in scrapbooks, opening mail, balancing the checkbook, folding laundry, or placing freshly ironed clothes to be put away. What greater place to wrap a pretty package?

◪ Hang a decorative painted tray on the wall.

◪ Place some colorful bottles on the window ledge. Toss in a daisy or two.

◪ Find an old, free-standing butcher block you actually use for chopping vegetables or preparing food.

◪ To warm up the feeling of a kitchen, have a variety of un-matched chairs, including a child's chair.

◪ Hang colorful plaid or striped cotton dish towels as curtains. Use 2-inch-wide grosgrain ribbons or cut up a dish towel for tabs; hang from ¾-inch dowels painted white, supported by white wooden brackets purchased at the hardware store.

◪ Have one china cupboard with clear glass doors. To show off your best dishes, hang simple decorative tiles on the back wall. If possible, install tiny Christmas tree lights under each shelf, hidden by a ¾-inch wooden strip.

◪ Keep several white Corian cutting boards handy next to the stove and sink.

▣   Treat yourself to a white sturdy garbage can. Use tall white Hefty Cinch Sak garbage bags with yellow drawstrings.

▣   Install a mirror on the back wall of a staging counter. This is ideal for candlelight kitchen buffet meals.

▣   Hang amusing trompe l'oeil dishes painted with fruits, vegetables, or other appetizing foods like croissants, caviar or cheese and crackers.

▣   Use a hanging rack for everyday dishes, including a collection of your favorite mugs.

▣   Put your wooden spoons in a decorative canister and have it near the stove.

▣   Hang a dried flower wreath on the wall.

▣   Have one cabinet to store liquor and mixes.

▣   Replace your old cabinet hardware with simple, shiny brass wire pulls 3 to 4 inches long.

▣   Buy a hand-held tile cutter and some tile glue, and set a border of decorative tiles as a back splash for your counters.

▣   Turn a built-in kitchen desk into a meaningful writing place. Set it up with a lamp, stationery, writing pads, and pens. There is something special about the atmosphere of a kitchen to a writer. Place a blotter pad over the surface to give yourself a spirit of place.

▣   Rethink the location of all your storage areas. Rearrange everything, based on use. Have one cabinet near the dishwasher for all the things you use every day from cereal bowls, to coffee mugs, to wineglasses. The fact that you have everything in limited quantity in one place makes setting up a breakfast tray a snap.

▨ Think of your kitchen as a café, a gathering place for fun and conversation. Food preparation is only one of the many functions of this room. Walk into your kitchen and see it with fresh eyes.

Chapter 9

FAMILY SPACES

We no longer have to go up to the attic or down to the basement to be with our children at home. They are welcome to join us wherever we are, whether it be in the living room, kitchen, terrace, or in our bedroom on Saturday morning. Today, in fact, there are few (if any) areas that are off limits for children. They want to be where the action is, and we want them with us. More and more, families are coming together in an informal room set aside for relaxation, recreation, and togetherness. Whether we call this space a den, family room, sunroom, sitting room, or playroom, this is the room in which we are most emotionally invested because it truly belongs to us all. It is where our most spontaneous living takes place.

These are the spaces that fully reveal the spirit and pulse of family life. Whereas the dominion of dollars expended will rarely draw us as a family to the living room—we may want our children there, but not their Popsicles and chocolate chip cookies—family rooms are the divining rods of domesticity. Increasingly, we recognize this central truth; and so the casual spaces we create—whether they are comfortably cozy or cathedral-ceiling modern—become all the more meaningful, functional, pleasant, and welcoming.

Take responsibility for the way your home feels.

Many first-time home buyers or young parents are drawn to houses where such potential exists. Their budgetary priorities often provide for interior renovations to expand an already existing family space, to build on a multiuse room, or to create the eating and family space widely known as a "California room." But a room that is initially planned to meet the requirements of small children will evolve naturally as the children mature and share this space with visiting friends. And when the children are gone, we recapture and adapt the space, once more transforming a room that has mirrored our life course.

In our house, the upstairs sitting room has become one of our favorite places to gather as a family. It amuses me to acknowledge this now because the room was initially so unattractive that we used it as an attic substitute when we were trying to settle the other parts of the house. The sitting room is square but not particularly graceful: Its two windows face south—and smack into our neighbor's windows. While the room has a woodburning fireplace and brick hearth and mantel, over time soot had caused the brick to become a grimy gray. It was almost as if the walls and trim had weathered to match it.

This spiritless room might well have remained an attic surrogate had I not received a phone call from a producer for Oprah Winfrey's show, inviting me to take a wreck of a room and transform it...in three days...for fifteen hundred dollars. The producer wondered if I would rise to the challenge and suggested she would have no trouble locating a real-life room for me to make over. When I mentioned that I had such a wreck right under my very own roof, we were on, and before I knew it, a camera crew was on its way to photograph the "before" shots.

After that, the three-day countdown began in earnest. With the help of Peter, my daughter Alexandra, and my assistant, Elisabeth, we worked feverishly to accomplish the transformation. All that we were required to do was to save our receipts to document that we hadn't exceeded the modest budget.

Friends are generous, wanting everything to come your way for you at home.

Privately, we affectionately refer to this room as the "Oprah" room, but in reality it is our sweet family sitting room. It is now a little gem, tucked in the middle of the upstairs.

We began by stripping the doors to reveal the natural eighteenth-century pine underneath. We painted the walls flat pink and ragged them white in high gloss so they appeared to twinkle. Next, we painted the ceiling Atmosphere Blue, like the sky, on which we then lightly sponged tones of yellow, pinks, whites, and blue, like delicate clouds. Then we stenciled some ribbons and flowers around the top of the walls in periwinkle blue, and created the feeling of Delft tiles around the raised-brick fireplace facing, by stenciling small, stylized tulips in blue.

A large chunk of our budget went for two wing chairs covered in a pink and white striped cotton and for a Chippendale camelback loveseat, purchased off the floor at a national furniture store chain. We hung one of my favorite quilts on the wall by sewing a band of Velcro into the top and by nailing a lattice strip on the wall, onto which we glued the other piece of Velcro.

The windows were fun to do. As I mentioned earlier when discussing living room window treatments, I bought blue and white plaid kitchen towels and made café curtains. I also cut up a pink and white kitchen towel and made tabs for the top of each curtain. At the lumberyard we purchased four 36-inch-long, ⅝-inch-diameter wood dowels, which we cut in half and painted white to form rods for hanging the curtains. By adjusting the height of the 2-inch tab headings, we were able to get away with not hemming the curtains to fit. It was instant gratification, and the entire cost for the two window treatments was under thirty dollars.

Finally, we found an old high cabinet in the basement that we also painted Atmosphere Blue and hand-painted some flowers gathered in ribbons on the front and sides — making a perfect place for books, the TV, or memorabilia.

We are drawn to this cozy, charming space more than we

A pine table is a proper thing, but a pine table that pretends to be black walnut is an abomination.
—Ella Church Rodman

I like things that look used, especially when they were used by someone who matters to me.
—Gary Hager, decorator

would ever have dreamed. We use the fireplace in the winter and gather here for conversation or reading. It has become a morning room as well as a place for quiet after-dinner activity.

The significant thing to remember when setting up your own family spaces is to keep designs simple and maintenance low. Because many family rooms have fireplaces, the single most important decision you will make is whether to orient your furniture toward it, or toward your television (or VCR and stereo). How are you going to house your home entertainment equipment? Does the room already have cabinetry? Or are you going to create built-ins? Will the room contain bookshelves? A table and chairs where you can gather to do a puzzle, homework, or special projects? Does a family member play a musical instrument? Is special lighting required, or window coverings to counter glare? Will there be a computer in this space?

One couple I know created a marvelous new family space by extending a sunroom that ran alongside their living room 25 feet farther into the backyard. This new room has windows on three sides and a lovely skylight. Built-in cabinetry separates a children's play area (where games, puzzles, and art supplies may be stored) as well as a built-in computer table where the boys do their homework. The seating area on the other side of the divide contains two contemporary salmon-colored loveseats, a chair and end table painted sand and turquoise, a sofa table behind the loveseats, and a pine coffee table covered with colorful enamel-framed family photographs and baskets of flowering plants. The loveseats face an angled corner cabinet, which stores the TV and VCR as well as assorted records, CDs, and tapes. The entire floor is covered in a soft, nubby beige carpet.

One of my favorite family spaces is a California-style room. The kitchen is open and connects visually to the furniture groupings beyond it by a painted, large-scale yellow and white checkerboard flooring. Harmonizing colors of fresh red, grass green, daffodil yellow, and indigo blue upholstery, pillows, and kitchen tile add to the open, airy effect.

For clients whose cathedral-ceiling family room was also dominated by a massive stone fireplace, the challenge was to select properly scaled furniture so that the room's architectural features wouldn't seem overwhelming. We did this by using two large rattan sofas and armchairs, generously cushioned; a splendid fruitwood game table; and colorful braided area rugs to define and anchor the furnishings. And for clients who wanted to create the feeling of a summer room in their family space, we installed terra-cotta–tiled flooring and two sets of French doors, and provided graceful white wicker furniture cushioned in soft, faded cotton pastels. A green and white sisal rug and lots of plants bring the garden indoors, making this room as comfortable as it is functional, all year round.

Your family space need not be reserved for family time only. It is a room designed for casual living, in which to congregate with our friends, and our children's friends. This is the room to make as down-to-earth as it can be — all the better for joining in the fun of Super Bowl Sunday, beer and pretzels, your children's skits, Chinese food on a Friday night. For it is down-to-earth living that makes our homes a continuous source of satisfaction.

Pleasant memorabilia of living —Ruby Ross Wood, describing the extraordinary atmosphere of time on earth

GRACE NOTES

▦ If you have small children, an apartment or a house should accommodate the entire family. Simplify your lifestyle during these important years.

▦ The family room should be comfortable and also look nice. Natural woven rattan furniture with soft, colorful, washable, loose cotton cushions are excellent choices. The furniture should be lightweight enough to move around.

▦ Area rugs are more practical for a room with multiple uses. A hardwood floor is best for Lego building blocks.

✸ As much as I resist the invasion of technology on our leisure time, I do love to curl up on the sofa with the family to watch an old movie on the VCR. This room shouldn't even attempt to hide all the equipment. It's the one room where you have something to plug in for everyone.

✸ Check to be sure you have four duplex outlets for all your equipment. If you have a telephone, a fax, and a copying machine, no matter who is home or what the activities, you can enjoy the company and still get some work done.

✸ There are many families in which reading is a far greater priority than watching television. What provisions you make for this is up to you to decide. Have a game table or card table where the whole family can work on a puzzle together.

✸ Some of my clients call their family space a music room to get the emphasis off watching television. Have a cabinet with drawers to store tapes and CDs.

✸ White or yellow walls are cheerful, even on rainy days. If the room has plywood paneling that closes the room in too much, you can have the wood pickled to lighten it without giving up the warm wood texture and grain.

✸ Track ceiling lights work well in this space for games and reading and don't take up any space in the room. One 8-foot track in the center of the ceiling can accommodate four light cans with up to 150 watts per fixture. Aim the cans where you want the most light.

✸ For the furniture, select a cotton print that is colorful but not so wild that you'll grow tired of it. Have all cushion and pillow covers close with Velcro so they can be machine washed. Use a preshrunk fabric. If possible, have a second set of cushion covers made so they can always be fresh and clean.

▦ Hide a roller shade behind a balloon shade at the window to darken the room easily for watching television or home movies.

▦ Build a 20-inch-deep windowseat. Install strips of wood in a latticework design to hide the radiator and air conditioner unit. Have a removable or hinged panel to allow access to air.

▦ Install a white ceiling fan to cool and refresh the room romantically and safely, and without noise.

▦ Build bookcases on either side of the window, from the floor to the top of the window trim. If any shelf is wider than 36 inches, reinforce it so it won't sag. Allow each family member to display personal treasures on his/her own shelf.

▦ Have a large, 30-inch-round ottoman where you can put up your feet. The ottoman should be 1 to 3 inches lower than the height of the sofa or chair seats. Install a swivel underneath for added fun.

▦ The coffee table has to be large enough to put a tray on it as well as provide room for newspapers, magazines, and flowers. Decorative ceramic tiles are a practical surface, as they can be wiped clean. Purchase a wicker table base and install tiles in place of the recessed glass top.

▦ Find an old wet bar that the children can enjoy as a soda fountain.

▦ Frame all the children's birthday party invitations using colored mats. Hang them together in a group.

⊞ Feel free to bring your exercise bike or NordicTrack into this room. Many people enjoy reading the newspaper while working out. We all need a space where we can come after jogging, still in our sweats, to grab a cool drink and flop into a chair and put our feet up.

⊞ Long after the children grow up and leave home, this room will be used as a place to relax in a casual atmosphere.

Chapter 10

THE STUDY

Everyone needs a private retreat from the world in which to read and write, to contemplate and appreciate. Just as the family pet goes to curl up where he feels secure and comfortable, so must we all have that special place where we can squeeze the essence of meaning from what we observe and experience; where we can shelter the letters, files, documents, and other assorted paperwork of our lives; a room where we can close the door to work or find solace and relief. It is a room we respond to individually, a home within our home.

If you are a writer, if you are attending school, if you are a minister, lawyer, banker, editor, or owner of a small business, your study becomes essential. A friend wrote her master's thesis at the secretary in her upstairs study. A minister prepares his sermons in a solarium-turned-study off the living room; and I know a woman, the full-time mother of active preschoolers, who has converted her third-floor attic into a studio where she writes and illustrates the children's books she someday hopes to publish. For all these people, studies are safe havens.

I am strong-minded about the need to claim a private place of your own—even if it is only the corner of an apartment. My readers have confirmed and affirmed my belief that this one, as-

Never take on a partner.
—Eleanor McMillen Brown

❖

sertive act can liberate your sense of pleasure and wonder at home. Whether it is an unused room over the garage, a grown child's room, the front hall closet (yes!), or a finished attic—you can conquer space and make it yours. Here, you can plan, think, read, write, sort through papers, putter, involve yourself in projects. There is no excuse for not creating a personal retreat, because it is within anyone's reach. It is a place of luminosity, enlightenment, and entitlement. It is your very own.

Peter and I have adjoining studies upstairs, a windfall, I confess, of finding ourselves empty nesters with rooms to spare. In our studies, we work independently, but side by side: There is no door between us, only a wooden saddle across the wide pine floorboards, and each space is very different, one from the other. But we share light from our five collective windows, the telephone, fax, and copying machine, pictures of family, friends, small favorite paintings, and, occasionally, afternoon tea.

How joyful it is to go there to have a moment's peace. Solitude is as important to me as company, but this is where I go to make notes, do research, write letters, write my books, and to think. There are no interruptions, no random noises. When I'm there, the door is (figuratively) closed and I am not home. Even though it is a tiny room, there is lots of space to spread out; and because it's mine, I'm free to use the floor to make piles and to sort papers into proper categories without any confusion from others. I can return to this space knowing that everything will be exactly as I left it; I can leave it assured that it will welcome my return. Even if you don't have a room you can use in precisely this way, you can accomplish the same thing by setting up a folding screen or partition.

The most important piece of furniture in a study is the desk. You may position it where you feel it gives you the best view and where you can take advantage of the light, although some people prefer to place their desks inward, against the wall, for a different kind of concentration. My desk is another provincial French farm table, a gift from Peter for our seventeenth wedding

For without the private world of retreat man becomes virtually an unbalanced creature.
—Eleanor McMillen Brown

anniversary. It is made of four smooth boards that probably came from the attic of a barn in Provence. The wood is pegged, and there are many worn holes and gaps between the boards. I sit there listening to the wind rustling in the trees, and I can hear the tick of a clock as my fountain pen scratches across the page.

Because studies are most often created out of a need for a place to go work, they are by nature usually utilitarian and neutral in decor. But this doesn't have to be the rule, particularly since studies are so singular and private. There is no question that the more we utilize a certain area of the home, the more personal it becomes. Peter and I recently went to visit a friend. In his attractive, hunter-green study, the furniture consisted of a large, comfortable desk, a chintz-upholstered reading chair and ottoman, a side table, bookcases, and a good reading light. Good reading light is actually a key factor in studies. In this room it was provided by a decorative desk lamp and a standing halogen lamp, which throws its beams up toward the ceiling, flooding the room with light.

Some studies are quite formal. Clients created distinctly different his and hers studies—hers was light and airy, with a fireplace, water lily chintz curtains, a loveseat, and a large, round ottoman, upholstered in the curtain fabric. The ottoman functioned as a table—books were stacked on it, and it could accommodate a marvelous silver tea tray from which she enjoyed serving guests. His study was very masculine. A sensuous burgundy print covered the chair to his highly polished mahogany partner's desk, and on the floor was a fine antique Aubusson rug with an eggplant-covered background. While this is a room where serious banker's thoughts take place, handsome framed wall prints and assorted memorabilia gave a warm and personal feeling.

The study is one room where furniture must be kept to a minimum. Here may be an excellent spot to install a wall system for books or files; but whatever you do, don't overdo. The ma-

Much of the character of everyman may be read in his house.
—John Ruskin

terials that seem most appropriate for studies are those that are comfortable to curl up and relax on. Many clients I have worked with also favor suede and leather. If you wish to bring splashes of bold color into the room, be sure to scale your fabric choice to the room's physical dimensions. Studies are often quite small; so if, for example, you have only one or two pieces of furniture to upholster, a small-scaled pattern will likely work best. You don't want to overwhelm the room, or yourself!

Peter and I put our respective studies to similar purposes, but they could not be more different. I call mine my "Zen room" and it's as light and spare as it can be, while his has lots of dark contrasting woods. My furnishings are quite spartan: a desk, a desk chair, which is actually a low, even rigid, school chair I picked up for fifteen dollars years ago in Santa Fe, and there's a bench on which I stack books, magazines, and manuscript boxes. Simple white-tab curtains hang at the windows, and a small geranium-red hooked rug (with my corporate signature swan spreading her wings) is the room's only colorful focal point.

Peter's study, on the other hand, is cluttered with the things he loves to have around him when he works: photographs of friends and colleagues, and a framed collection of letters hangs on the walls; clocks, books, and music boxes adorn his desk. His floor is covered with a Finnish rag rug of soft blues that complements the blue and white woven-textured seat cushion of his high ladderback desk chair. While my study is an ode to tranquillity and space, his is a fugue to chaos! But our different spaces work for us.

Of all the rooms in your house, the study should inspire you to feel your best to do your best work. Invest in a pretty table on which to place your computer, if you use one, and an extra-thick door to shut out the sounds of family life. Consider purchasing a chaise longue and attractive decorative boxes and baskets to hold your desk and writing implements. Bring soothing music into this room, pictures and postcards to inspire you,

There are a great many things better than gold.
—*Justice Oliver Wendell Holmes*

and a vase of shrimp-colored tulips. Spray-paint file cabinets in your favorite color. It is, after all, your room. Make it as calming to the spirit as a long walk in the woods and as stimulating as the summer sun, a room that speaks to you. And when you are there, you will know that you've truly come home.

GRACE NOTES

■ The best way to decorate the study is with books. If the room doesn't have bookcases, locate a place where you can add them. If you have a lot of books, the shelves can extend from the baseboard to the ceiling molding. If there's no closet in the study and you have a lot of supplies that require storage, consider installing cabinets below the bookcases.

■ Fill a high piece or a corner piece with some of your most treasured books. Paint the inside back of the cabinet Wharf Green, Fuller O'Brien 1-E-77, Lafayette Blue 1-D-37, or Yellow Crayon 1-A-28.

■ Find a spot for an old-fashioned Lawson loveseat with scroll arms. It will be ideal for reading, and makes a cozy place for two.

■ This room is perfect for displaying sentimental photographs, memorabilia, and favorite treasures. Consider hanging black-and-white photographs on the walls. Put a fragment of decorative carving or some pictures over the doors.

■ Paint a less-than-perfect coffee table the same color as the walls of the room, stack it high with books, and your eye won't notice that it is less than ideal.

※ This is one room you might consider painting a dark, rich color. You don't need an expensive paneled room for it to feel serious. I created two small studies out of maid's rooms in our New York City apartment, for example. They're small, private rooms that inspire me to study. Manor Green, Fuller O'Brien 1-E-128 semi-gloss, or Red Geranium 1-C-120 semi-gloss can turn a nondescript space into something quite elegant.

※ When the color of the walls is extremely rich and dark, the room needs some relief. Bleach and stain a natural tone in the floor in 12-inch squares, creating a checkerboard design on your regular floorboards.

※ Place two-drawer lateral metal file cabinets along one wall. Paint them to match the walls. Place a 2-inch-thick bull-nose–edged (½-inch-round edge) piece of natural oak over the cabinets, and coat it with polyurethane.

※ Build an upper section to hold books with adjustable shelves 15 inches deep. Allow 20 to 22 inches from the top of the file cabinets to the bottom of the bookshelves so you have plenty of work space.

※ Install a strip for small incandescent bulbs under the bookcases to illuminate the work ledge.

※ In a small room, rather than having a tiny desk, run a 2-inch-thick oak bull-nose ledge, 36 inches deep, the full length of the room, supported by heavy-duty angle irons, which can also be painted in the same shade as your wall color.

※ Above your work space, have a carpenter build a wall of cubbyholes 8 inches deep in which to store reference books, file cards, stationery, and notebooks. Store what you use every day on lower surfaces. Fifteen inches above the work ledge at the bottom of the cubicles, install a series of drawers measuring 14 inches wide by 4 inches high with incandescent light strips underneath.

▦ Track lighting is extremely useful because you can aim the cans at specific work areas in the room.

▦ In a small room, consider having one generous partner's desk rather than two smaller desks, which are less efficient because they don't provide enough work space to spread out on.

▦ If you use a computer, keep it on a separate stand so that the desk area will be for research and study.

▦ When we study, we all love to lean back in our chair and put our feet up on a footstool. A stool is also a convenient place to rest a snack tray.

▦ Try to keep your desk surface clear when it's not in use, except for a lamp and a few favorite objects that inspire you to work. There are several antique brass cups on my desk filled with my pen collection. I also keep a letter rack on the desk so I can gaze at a Claude Monet postcard. I keep a Venetian glass paperweight in front of me as I work, to play with between thoughts.

▦ Light a candle and place a fresh flower bud vase to keep you company while you try to do your best work.

▦ Your study is an ideal place for a beautiful old clock because the ticking rhythm is soothing.

▦ When we study, we're often contemplative and look up from work for inspiration. Have a favorite painting near your desk.

◈ In addition to photographs of family and friends on the walls, frame some meaningful letters you've received, or a copy of a famous historical letter written by someone you admire.

◈ Near your desk—in a stack or between bookends—keep a dozen or so books that have had the greatest impact on you. What kinds of books will they be? Are many of them by the same author? Are they contemporary or classic books?

◈ Let your study become a guest room. What could be a greater compliment to your friends than to stay in such an intimately personal room.

◈ Every once in a while, when you discover a book that means a lot to you, treat yourself by having it leather bound.

◈ Of all the rooms in your house, allow your study to be the most sentimental, revealing all your varied interests and achievements since childhood. This is the room that is tailor-made for you!

Chapter 11

YOUR BEDROOM

Bedrooms are the most revealing of our personalities. Here we lie down and shut our eyes, lower our defenses, and open ourselves to dreams, fantasies, and love. The intimacy of this room makes it a space that is highly charged emotionally. When we love, we go to bed. When we sleep, we are in bed. When we are sick, whether in mind, body, or spirit, we take to the bed. We are restored by bed rest. Our bedroom is where we experience ecstasy, or great sadness. It is the room where we very often receive fateful telephone calls, bearing the bad as well as the good news. It is where the joys of life and its sorrows are deeply lived and felt. Think about the reality of your own life and what this room has meant to you.

I have loved bedrooms all my life, beginning when I was five and staying in the guest room at the home of my godmother. This special room had a fireplace, and I would sit on the great four-poster bed Indian-style, rapt in joy, and stare into the crackling fire she would lay for me on cold New England mornings. The power of suggestion is strong and left me with a passionate craving to have one day a bedroom with its own wood-burning fireplace.

Love of beauty and the desire to create it is a primal instinct of man.
—*Eleanor McMillen Brown*

When Peter and I bought our house, it was good fortune that one of the five fireplaces was in our bedroom. But we were told this fireplace could not operate because the house furnace took up the flue. When I heard this news, I tried to be brave. Unbeknownst to me, Peter took aside our contractor and instructed him to hire the best mason in the area to try to rework the flue to make the fireplace work. The mason apparently knew how to cantilever the flue, French style, so that it would draw. The chimney would have to be enlarged, and while I was out of town on a book tour, the mason did his magic. The night I returned, Peter ran up to the bedroom, laid the fire, and lit it before I came up the back stairs. Peter stood in front of the door, kissed me, and moved away to reveal the roaring fire. "Surprise!"

There are no words to convey my delight, or to explain the joy this gesture of love continues to give me. In the morning, instead of turning up the heat, we sit together in the room and talk over our coffee, and at night we can read and have a conversation before we turn out the lights. I don't think we've missed having a fire there every morning and evening except during the muggy weather of midsummer. No one has ever seen this fireplace lit, except us. This is something we share privately.

Dreams can come true and bedrooms are the place to make them real. Clients inquire, "Where do I begin?" and always want to know "Where is the best place to put the bed?" The bed, of course, is the largest piece of furniture in the room and should be placed where you feel the most comfortable. Usually there is a tension between wanting to utilize a view as fully as possible and desiring privacy from neighbors. Decorators will tell you to place the bed where it looks best when you enter the room — usually in the middle of your longest wall.

Had Peter and I followed this rule in our house, we would not have been able to enjoy both our view of the water and of the fire. So we placed the bed two feet off-center, where we can sit and watch the boats, or snuggle under the blankets, the room illuminated by the pink flickering glow of late-evening flames.

We cannot do better than to accept the standards of other times, and adapt them to our uses.
—Elsie de Wolfe

When there is a good reason for something to be placed where it is, it usually works.

By having the bed off-center, we are able to have a large armoire in the corner and still have room for Peter's large end table that holds his mountain of bedside reading. There is no air conditioner in this room, and so we have a ceiling fan centered on the bed. By alternating the four speeds, we feel we are getting sea breezes. It causes the white cotton swags and bed hangings to rustle.

One of the most peculiar aspects of our bedroom is that directly opposite the fireplace, and behind our bed, there is a door to the sitting room. Instinctively, we hung a quilt over the back headpost to conceal it. Then we realized how pretty the views from both rooms looked without it, and we decided to take the quilt down. Now, we have a sweeping view of the upstairs, all bathed in light and freshness. Our decision was unconventional to be sure—risky and idiosyncratic—but if you can't please yourself in your bedroom, where else can you?

By opening up the bedroom to this small sitting room, our four bedroom windows have grown to six—and more. That is, we wanted even more light, and so we asked an artist to hand-paint some sash window frames with pastel tints of flowers and leaves into which we then installed mirrored panes. We hung these mirror frames horizontally in the corner to the left of my bedside table; they act as windows, bring in more light and different views of the water. We hung a few additional sash mirrors about the room, giving the appearance of a generously windowed space; and even the oval mirror on the armoire door gives an impression of windows because of the actual windows it reflects.

As you focus on your own bedroom scheme, remember that the key walls are the one behind your bed and the one you stare at while in bed. If you like mirrors, the latter is the perfect wall to hang one on, as the mirror will take this wall and push it back visually. If your bedroom windows are close together, consider

When is the last time your room laughed?

putting a mirror between them to add softness and to create the impression of a larger window area. Your bedroom walls are also a good place to display some refreshing piece of art, such as a nice landscape. It will give you the feeling of being in a beautiful place when you wake up. In any case, I do feel that the plainer the bedroom walls are, the better. You want the room to have the flexibility to accommodate pictures, mirrors, and fancy, colorful bedding.

Because some of our bedroom floorboards are as wide as 14½ inches, we love having them bare, with a few small rag rugs scattered about. Carpeting in bedrooms, however, is practical, especially in colder climes, as it warms up the room, feels good against your bare feet, and is an excellent sound absorber. A small room also appears larger when carpeted.

When selecting your carpeting, remove your shoes and stockings and walk on it to be sure it is soft. Choose a low pile; shaggy rugs get dirty quickly. The height of the pile isn't as important as its quality. Be careful that your carpet isn't a track for footprints. Friends spent some good money on a new bedroom carpet that has to be vacuumed daily. And if you choose a patterned carpet, take care that it doesn't upstage your bed. In fact, before you commit to a carpet, go to the linen closet with a carpet sample and make sure it coordinates with your sheets.

The colors of our bedroom are important, and while I've worked with just every imaginable color scheme, blue is still the most popular, perhaps because it is so soothing and contemplative. Whatever you decide upon, try to have clarity in all your colors. For one client—who did favor blue—we used a high-gloss enamel white trim, a cool, pale Brittany blue for the walls, and a softer Atmosphere Blue on the ceiling. The curtains and bedding are of hand-painted irregular white stripes on blue canvas; the curtains hang from white wooden rings on shiny white poles. The wood pieces in the room are blond, and the room looks clean, crisp, and pleasant.

Everything in a bedroom should contribute to an atmosphere of peace.
—Billy Baldwin

Another favorite blue bedroom is a graciously scaled square room with two large picture windows overlooking New York City's Central Park and reservoir. These clients live high-powered professional lives, and their apartment has many stimulating spaces. But their blue bedroom was created for a soothing, calming effect. Here, too, we painted the walls blue and the trim white, but used blue and white cotton chintz curtains in a geometric print, a woven blue cotton print for a chair and ottoman, and a dark blue textured print for the husband's reading chair. To bring the outdoors in, we placed a huge ficus tree between the two windows, and it thrives in all the natural light. At night, a floor can, hidden behind a terra-cotta pot, lights up the tree for added atmosphere.

One of the reasons this room is such a success is because there is a variety of blues, which keeps it from looking dull and monochromatic. We combined cool blues for the wool rug, walls, and curtains, but the print on the chair and ottoman introduces some turquoise. There is a blue plaid lap blanket on the husband's chair, and a mohair blanket of five different blues, a touch of soft pink, and a few strands of yellow for the wife to snuggle up to. A few finishing touches of red — a tea table and tray and some lacquered boxes — help to warm up the room. It's hard to imagine a more comforting retreat than this peaceful haven ten floors above the noisy city.

Another client, also a city person, has heavily padded fabric-stretched walls of soft peach, which help reduce outside noise. The same peach shade covers her modern white bed, an upholstered chaise, and simple Roman shades. There seems to be a trend, I have found, toward creating simple, serene bedrooms where we can rebalance ourselves.

As you consider your room furnishings, always try to weigh comfort with aesthetics. Since the bed is the focal point of any bedroom, and the place where you spend most of your time, buy the best mattress you can. Back problems are rampant; and you'll

Concentrate on intrinsic values.
—Stanley Barrows

do better with a firm mattress. What you place your mattress on is up to you. If you own an old family bed, or a beautiful new one, it may be an odd size, in which case your mattress will have to be custom-made. If the room is small, you may want to select a low platform bed in order to make the room appear larger. Once the bed height is determined, everything else in this room can be scaled to this measurement.

Headboards serve the practical purpose of giving us something on which to rest our heads so we won't soil the wall. Here you have a wide variety of creative solutions to choose from. You may desire a lovely, antique wood headboard. Or you might prefer an upholstered one, which you can make by using plywood and foam padding with a favorite fabric stapled over it, much like the stretched canvas used by artists. (If you use an upholstered headboard, invest in extra material so you can change it if it becomes dirty.) I've also seen some marvelous headboards created from the most unlikely materials. One couple purchased, and cut down, a wrought-iron gate that had once been in the front yard of a Welsh cottage; while another couple wall-mounted antique wood panels behind their bed. The possibilities are truly endless.

End tables next to the bed are useful and handy for keeping books, magazines, clock, and telephone at arm's reach. While the tables should never match rigidly, they should complement each other. If you have the space, your end tables can be large, but they should always be in scale with the bed. Consider skirting an inexpensive circular table made of wallboard; skirted tables give you lots of underneath storage space and can hide clutter during the day. You can even hide a file cabinet under the table. Try using a pretty desk as an end table. The desk drawer can be extremely useful.

One of our bedroom walls cried out for a high piece of furniture, and we found a simple Irish pine cupboard with glass doors that fit the bill beautifully. When we put this cupboard in

Dream delivers us to dream, and there is no end to illusion.
—Ralph Waldo Emerson

place, I had no idea what we would put inside it; all I knew was that the piece felt right. But once I painted its back wall light blue, I realized that whatever I put in it would look splendid. At first, my journals and box collections, marbleized-covered writing books and binders went inside the piece as well as stationery and postcards, and then — voila! — after a short time I had something that not only looked wonderful but was also pure me.

About the television. Had our cupboard been an armoire or a linen press, we might have considered hiding the TV there when we weren't using it. But the cupboard's glass doors prohibited that, and, as it happens, we rarely watch TV anyway. But if you enjoy watching television, decide where you want to put it when you position your bed.

Somewhere in your bedroom there should be a comfortable chair or (if space allows) a small sitting area that includes a loveseat and low table. If closet space is at a premium, and you and your spouse require dressers, be sure that they are of different vintages to avoid that "matchy-matchy" motel look. Dressers, of course, provide good surface areas on which to display your favorite objects.

Surround yourself with things that mean something special to you.

One friend took this a step further and created a beautiful dressing table for herself, on which she has arranged collections of antique glass, silver-backed combs and brushes, and small silver bowls of potpourri on either side of the dressing table's pretty frosted glass-globed lamps.

Bedroom lighting should be relaxing and, like your living room, there should be lots of it coming from several different sources. The most flexible and practical lights for reading in bed are swing-arm wall lights, which keep your end table surfaces free. Good lighting to dress by, especially inside your clothes closet, is essential. And because the bedroom is your special area, the lights should be flattering. I recommend incandescent bedroom lighting.

Finally, consider your bedding. Do you get up in the morning, make the bed right away, and not get back in it again until evening? Do you flop on your bed whenever you have a minute? Do you make telephone calls while in bed? Read on top of it? Your answers to these questions will determine what fabrics you use.

Let's talk about sheets. Bedrooms are for pleasure, so make sure your sheets feel as good as they look. You may decide to forego bedspreads, which can be bulky and heavy, and go for an "unmade" look, splurging on pretty sheets and blanket covers. Sheets can be sewn together to cover blankets, but remember that any material that isn't quilted will wrinkle easily.

I am, as I've said before, a sucker for a beautiful quilt. Indeed, my passion for using quilts decoratively has gone far beyond the limits of the bedroom. Good quilts can be expensive, but you can often find bargains at country fairs. My clients almost always find quilts colorful, timeless, and comforting emotionally, and the bedroom is the most logical place to use them. A pink and white bedroom I love has a white bridal quilt on the bed and a pink and white patchwork quilt folded at the foot for a spontaneous nap. If you have a four-poster bed, you can hang a quilt on the back wall; the bedposts make a wonderful frame. If you own several bed quilts, interchange them frequently when you change the linens.

Quilts can be a connecting touch of Americana to any bedroom. For an art-collecting client I used a lemon–peel yellow silk-taffeta fabric that was intensified by the room's white walls, and placed a quilt at the end of a double chaise longue to soften this formal space. The quilt's design complemented the Portuguese bedroom rug, with its raspberry flowers interlaced with a yellow trellis design. And that Manhattan power couple's multiblue bedroom also benefited from blue and white quilted pillows. Their "unmade" bed was most elegant with fine blue and white flowered sheets with blue borders and scalloped edges. We placed a blue and white quilt on the bed and another on a bench nearby.

The most charming style is devoid of pretension.

To finish a bed, use lots of decorative pillows of varying sizes, whether they be shams, bedrolls, or baby pillows. You can edge them with old lace, or cover them, as I once did, with smocking material I saved from my little girls' outgrown dresses. The more pillows you have, the more sensuous your bed will look.

When you have a pretty bedroom, you can make more of it than just a room to sleep in. Peter and I spend time together in bed, reading, writing, and talking. We have juice and coffee in bed every morning. No matter how early we have to leave for an appointment in New York, or to catch the train back from Connecticut, we set our alarm clock way ahead so we can have private time before the day begins.

People often ask me what my favorite room is in my home. I always say that it's my romantic, pastel bedroom. We have everything here—our beautiful, white eyelet–swagged four-poster bed; good reading light; an abundance of quilts; a small painted chest at the foot of the bed stacked with books and magazines; a hand-painted breakfast tray; family photographs; favorite objects everywhere; and we have each other.

One of the problems with any room that has to be decorated is that we think it has to be picture perfect. In bedrooms, especially, we have to resist that impulse. We need to understand and identify with our surroundings. We want them to be beautiful and to inspire us, because beauty always shapes our mood and attitude. But there should be a generous amount of friendly clutter in the bedroom because we do so much good living there.

Your bedroom is not only the place where you are most vulnerable and receptive; it is also where you can maintain yourself in excellent company, on your own terms. Here you can be surrounded by your comforts, and be enriched by memories and personal delights. For Peter and me, the bedroom is a safe haven, where we allow life's mysteries to enlarge our capacity to hope and where we deepen our reverence for living. Bedrooms house our innermost feelings and provide a regular place of contentment, no matter how harsh the realities of the outside world. We

The most luxurious bedrooms have as little dressing equipment as possible.
—Billy Baldwin

come and go in the rhythms of energy and fatigue, one day lived and one yet to be lived. Here, in this mysteriously powerful room we can create a sacred place, a cocoon, just with a pretty bed, flowers, and lots of fresh air and light.

GRACE NOTES

※ No room is architecturally perfect. Place the bed where you have the most beautiful view and also the most privacy. Don't be concerned whether the bed is centered in the room, or how the bed appears from the doorway—once the door is shut you are in your private world.

※ Your bedroom is the most romantic room in the house. Soft pastel colors are enjoyed by men and women equally.

※ A four-poster bed makes you feel romantic, private, and special. Keep the bedposts plain or swag the top with simple white dotted swiss fabric. To avoid sewing, cut a 20-yard bolt in two. Start at one post, leaving 6 inches on the floor that you can tuck under, and drape the fabric in swags over the beam that connects the posts.

※ Shutters provide plenty of privacy, yet don't shut out the light when open.

※ To give a feeling of a sunny day in Bermuda, bleach the hardwood floors to look like the sand.

※ Create an inviting soft bed by using lots of decorative pillows, pretty sheets, and a quilt as a bed coverlet.

※ Rather than a large rug, most of which stay's hidden under the bed, use small colorful cotton rag rugs like bright beach towels in the sand. Placed on either side of the bed, they are soft, warm, and cozy to the bare foot.

※ Create a small sitting area containing a loveseat, a few chairs, and a tea table where you can sit, read, and enjoy your morning coffee.

※ Paint the ceiling flat Atmosphere Blue, Fuller O'Brien 1-D-47.

※ Always have fresh-cut flowers or a flowering plant to create an indoor garden for your private sanctuary.

※ Combine a mixture of pine, maple, and white wicker to create a nostalgic country mood.

※ Your bedroom is the ideal place for your favorite family photographs. With a variety of inexpensive stationery store frames, you can mat each picture with simple colorful marbleized paper from an art supply store.

※ Hand-paint some pastel flowers on a white wicker bed tray to keep beside the bed when not in use. When something is pretty, it shouldn't be hidden.

※ Paint your walls soft Beauty Pink, Fuller O'Brien 1-C-23, with semi-gloss white enamel paint trim.

※ Colorful boxes are wonderful for storing your files and can be easily and inexpensively made by covering ordinary shoeboxes and dress boxes in fabric or wallpaper.

▦ The most important place for a favorite painting is opposite the bed, so you can awaken to it, and it will be the last impression you have before you go to sleep.

▦ Just for fun, stack a table at the foot of the bed with art, architecture, and gardening books. This would also be a great spot for a little bouquet of tulips or daisies.

▦ In the winter, for a warm, cozy feeling drape your round bedside table with a white or pastel floor-length tablecloth. Add a square of your favorite chintz fabric to the top for extra color. Let the square overhang 6 to 12 inches.

▦ Because we spend more than a third of our lives in bed, collect a wardrobe for your bed: Invest in a variety of different sets of sheets, pillow shams, and blanket covers and an assortment of colorful patterned baby pillows and neck rolls.

▦ For reading in bed, contemporary functional halogen Tizio swing-arm lamps give excellent light and versatility. Another successful solution is to install a pair of wall-mounted swing-arm lamps with a three-way switch. They can be swung away from the bed when not in use.

▦ Fill a small lap desk with your favorite writing essentials so you can curl up in bed and catch up on your correspondence.

▦ Install a 14-inch-deep window ledge under your windows extending the entire length of the wall with space for generous bookcases below.

▦ The top of the window ledge can hold additional books, magazines, and other reading material.

▓ Locate a large rectangular basket with a handle to store half-read newspapers. I found a ten-dollar basket, 15 inches by 20 inches by 9 inches high, I spray-painted it white, and hand-painted pastel flowers and ribbons on it.

▓ Men and most women like blue bedrooms because the color is so soothing. Paint the walls flat Mystic Blue, Fuller O'Brien 1-D-74, and the bookcases and all trim semi-gloss white. Paint the ceiling one part flat Mystic Blue and three parts flat white enamel.

▓ If you want wall-to-wall carpeting, select a flat loop in a small overall geometric pattern in blue with white, green with white, or pink with white.

▓ Place a simple white ceiling fan over the bed to ensure comfort in all seasons. When the fan is on high speed, it makes the bed hangings rustle.

▓ If you're short on closet space, use a beautiful pine armoire, which also adds height and a focal point to the room.

▓ As each couple tends to choose their own favorite side of the bed, they should also have an end table that reveals their own personal style as well as accommodates their needs.

▓ Keep a small fabric-lined basket on your end table for necessary paraphernalia—scissors, paper clips, pens, ink cartridges, letter opener, stamps, lip gloss, body cream, Life Savers. Have the fabric overlap to cover the top of the table.

▓ A picture of yourself as a child in the bedroom will bring back happy memories.

▦ Mirrors are functional as well as aesthetically pleasing. Consider hanging several decorative mirrors in order to reflect your pretty room.

▦ Place some favorite floral potpourri on the window ledge.

▦ Stock up on favorite scented candles to soothe you while adding warmth and color to the room.

Chapter 12

CHILDREN'S ROOMS

When it comes to our children, we all want to do the right thing and make the right choices for them. But when it comes to their bedrooms, we can do best by taking our lead from their cues. That is, we should begin by recognizing that a child's room belongs to the child, and that it should reflect his/her personality, not ours.

Think of this room as a space to grow in, and consider ways of decorating the room so that it will serve your child's real needs. The way we approach the decorating can positively affect a child's physical and emotional development. The "pretty" room a parent might envision could be contrived and rigid, limiting the creativity and spontaneity of a child in search of himself. Children have their own timetables, which are different from ours, and so their room designs must consider that evolving person. Certainly, when we are preparing a baby's first room, the aesthetic choices we make will be our own; but once a child has moved beyond the nursery stage, he is old enough to participate in the decision-making process that involves the creation of his private world.

This is a truth I learned firsthand several years ago when I attempted to gain some precious extra storage space in our New

Beautiful birds build tasty nests.
—O. S. Fowler

York apartment. The logical solution (or so I thought) would be to expand our bedroom closet by extending it a few feet into the adjoining room, which happened to belong to the teenage Brooke. When I presented my plan to her ("Don't you have a beautiful new closet of *your* own? Won't your room still be plenty big?") Brooke burst out, "Mom. You don't understand! This is not my *room*. This is my world."

In the next few moments, she explained to me how she had created different rooms within her room. She had a place to study and to dress, to sleep and to do her schoolwork. All the different parts of her life required storage—her art supplies, books, sports equipment, and clothes—and she needed every square inch. "You have the living room and the library, your office and the hall, the kitchen and closets all over the apartment. My entire life is contained in this one room."

As they say, out of the mouths of babes.

Good design, functional furniture, color, and intelligently planned space are as important for children as they are for grown-ups. Elsewhere in this book I have made my case as to why rooms must never be allowed to become stage sets, and why they must grow and change as we do. This notion is perhaps nowhere else as important as in children's room design, because today's infant is tomorrow's preschooler—and next year's teenager. The years go by so fast, and while the actual space your child inhabits may stay the same, the child inhabiting it will not. The room will start out with a crib, which soon gives way to a single bed. But before long, your child will require extra sleeping arrangements for the overnight guest. Whether you'll want to buy a trundle bed, a double-decker, twin beds, a futon, or a sleeping bed is up to you. But eventually, you must decide, and you'll have to plan for it.

Similarly, you have to assess your long-range plans in other ways. Does your house have enough bedrooms for all the children you eventually intend to put in them? Will each child have his own room, or will he have to share one? Will it remain that

Home is a place of comfort and joy, like a warm coat on a cold night.

way until the time comes when an older child requires privacy, or when boys and girls need separate rooms? It's never too early to think about these questions: Their answers will inform your master plan. You may decide to turn the master bedroom over to the children, or to turn a finished attic over to a teenager. Certainly, when our children are small, we want to keep them near us. But later they, or we, may want a different kind of arrangement.

Our ideas about what's appropriate for children's rooms has also changed. Years ago, when I was first starting out in the business, decorators created very different rooms for boys and girls. In most cases, the girls' bedrooms were fluffy and in pastel shades, and the boys' were masculine and primary-colored. To-day, we know that rooms need not hold to such arbitrary gender differentiation. In fact, the trend seems to be toward more tailored spaces that are both flexible and spontaneous celebrations of that growing child.

Whenever I decorate for children, I always like to speak with them personally and to draw them out about the things they love. With five-year-old Kelly and nine-year-old Sarah, the result of each interview led to some imaginative designs.

Kelly showed me a picture she had made of a house with white shutters and a pink roof! She told me about her cat and that her favorite food was cantaloupe, her favorite color, lilac. She showed me her hair ribbon collection and her favorite bed-time book, a story about a bluebird and a yellow canary. When I asked her to close her eyes and to tell me what she saw, she replied, "A canopy bed, like my mommy and daddy's." And so when I set out to design her bedroom, these favorite things were factored into the mix. The canopied bed is done in a simple fresh chintz of lilac and cantaloupe, which came with a matching wallpaper; and we were able to top the bed with its own pink "roof." We put white plantation shutters at the windows and found a patchwork quilt for the end of the bed that not only picked up

What pictures don't show is the way music makes it all work.
— Jorge Silvetti, architect

the pastel tones of the walls and bedding, but also the blue and yellow that would remind her of her beloved bedtime book.

Sarah's vision was of a winter wonderland, and so we hung sheer white curtains at her windows, topped by ice-blue cotton valances. Her walls are delicately sponged in the same soft ice blue, and the painted floor creates the impression of a skating ring. Her child-sized sleigh bed is covered in white eyelet; and we painted a simple country cupboard in pale blue, with tiny Hans Brinker-like winter scenes.

Run with the imagination of your children. The fabric and wall-covering manufacturers are right there with you, whether a child's fancy takes him from teddy bears and school buses to rocket ships and rock stars. The important thing to remember is to scale your choices to the room's proportions (children's bedrooms are usually small), and you may want to paint the walls instead of papering them, and use decorative, illustrated borders. Remember, too, that if you're partial to wallpaper, you may have to change it as your child gets older. Personally, I prefer simple, clean painted walls in neutral colors—the better against which to hang Plexiglas-framed artwork. These may be changed regularly, just as art galleries create new exhibits. Or you can hang huge bulletin boards on the walls, and paint the doors and trim a bright color.

There was a period when my girls liked to have a roll of shelf paper on the walls over which they painted fantasy murals, which could also be changed. But if you do prefer a more orderly wall decoration and have some artistic talent, create (for commission) your own wall mural—a jungle scene or a night sky—and, if possible, have your child join in the project. By and large, however, the rule of thumb is that children's rooms are action-filled. Toys, games, books, trophies, and stuffed animals make a room *look* busy, and infuse it with their own color accents. So keep your schemes simple, and always remember that you'll have to make changes later on.

It takes great passion and great energy to do anything creative.
— Agnes DeMille

Earlier in the book, I discussed my personal design trinity of simplicity, appropriateness, and beauty. Children's rooms embody this principle, too. It's appropriate, for instance, to keep the floor surface unencumbered. Wall-to-wall carpeting interferes with child's play: Just try building a castle, playing jacks, or racing toy cars over a carpet. Carpets also show dirt, ink, and crumbs, accidents, and spills. Area rugs, on the other hand, can be rolled up and are easier to maintain. I love painted floors in children's rooms—I've seen some spectacularly inventive floor designs. But don't consider doing this unless you are willing to do the job right—lots of coats of paint and then a coat of polyurethane, as this type of floor gets hard wear and you don't want the paint to chip or flake.

Window treatments in children's rooms should also be simple. There is an impulse to overdo a little girl's room with heavy valances and poufy curtains. Instead, I suggest using decorative shades (which may be laminated from the bedroom fabric you've selected) or straight-hanging curtains. A child should be able to look out at the world.

Look up!

❖

Children should have a growing system of furniture that builds as their needs change. Think in terms of modular building blocks, scaled for small people, designed for easy operation, and that are sturdy, plain, and easily managed. Children should be encouraged to be self-sufficient. If they can't open their clothing drawers or reach a hanging garment without having to ask for help, what kind of message are you sending them? Double-pole the closets (and switch the hangers around when the season changes). And if it's important that even a small child make his bed in the morning, make sure that he or she can manage. Comforters can be for now; bedspreads may have to wait.

Storage space should be plentiful, safe, *and* accessible. You can devise imaginative and inexpensive solutions. I know a woman who painted and decorated an old steamer trunk as a birthday gift to her daughter. The trunk holds all her daughter's dress-up clothes, costume jewelry, and pocketbooks. Another woman painted wooden doorknobs in high-gloss primary colors and screwed them at 1-foot intervals into a wall in her son's room. He hangs his growing collection of baseball caps, knapsacks, mitts, and binoculars from them. And because children are natural collectors, be sure to have ample surface area for their boxes and small jars.

Children's rooms can and should be fanciful. You can take a simple set of chairs and a table and paint them in wild stripes and geometric designs, and fit the tabletop with a Lucite cover. You can also take the most humble furniture set, remove the hardware, and replace it with painted, high-gloss plywood that you've cut into the shapes of stars or small animals, which you can screw back over simple drawer pulls. Spray-paint your grandmother's wrought-iron bed in gunmetal gray. Or, if you are handy with a needle and thread, you can create a fabulous headboard and footboard using plywood and foam padding, much as I discussed in Chapter 11: Create a little "house" at the head, with a picket fence and flowers at the foot, or even a racing car.

Children sense instinctively when they are respected and when their feelings and opinions mean something to a parent. So ask them questions, show them color chips and fabric swatches, and let them tell you about their favorite things. Children want to express a personal point of view. We want them to be pleased with the results, and to say to their friends (and ours), "Come see my room." This is the space that molds and supports your child in the best and most profound sense. Allow the vibrancy of his/her personality to guide you in that natural direction. The greatest gift you can give your child is a sense of empowerment. Moreover, by allowing your child to live that creative process with you, you are teaching him to take responsibility for his own life designs and to care responsibly for whatever he helped choose, and the design he helped create.

Bold, exciting; full of life and vibrating with color
—Dorothy Draper

GRACE NOTES

※ Change is the only constant in a child's room. Nothing can stay in scale or be useful unless it is capable of adapting. As the child grows, the room must grow also.

※ Adults have many rooms in their lives, but a child usually has one or a portion of one. Let this space be everything it can be to your child.

※ Children don't appreciate expensive rooms. A roll of shelf paper attached to the wall with some colorful Magic Markers will mean more (for the first twelve years, at least) than some expensive, fragile wallpaper.

※ By the time a child is two, let him or her choose favorite colors for the room, preselected by you.

※ The sooner a child learns how to make a choice and then see the results, the easier it will be for him to make meaningful personal decisions later on in life.

※ When two children share a room, locate two distinct, private corners for each child. The center can be a shared play-living space.

※ A wooden or cork floor is preferable to wall-to-wall carpeting because it isn't fair for a child to have to be responsible for keeping some impractical carpeting spot-free. The floor has to be cleanable, no matter how great the disaster.

※ Avoid putting a crib on an exterior wall because this is the coldest wall in the room.

▦ Storage areas should be geared to the age and height of the child in order to foster self-sufficiency. Put the clothes rod on an adjustable shelf bracket so it can be raised as the child grows.

▦ Encourage a child to record his/her room decoration and transformation with an instant camera and mount the pictures in a scrapbook.

▦ Place the child's artwork in inexpensive clear plastic frames of various sizes purchased at art supply stores.

▦ Hang an indoor window box so your child can experience the wonder of nature year round.

▦ White high-gloss walls are ideal for a child's room because they are scrubbable, they reflect light, and they are good for hanging posters and bulletin boards.

▦ Ceiling track lighting works well for children because it is safe, effective, and can be targeted at work and play zones.

▦ Set up an easel near the window with a large pad and a supply of colored Magic Markers. Encourage your child to sign and date each work of art.

▦ Construct a platform eight inches higher than the floor. Cover it in industrial flat-loop carpeting to make an area where children can build as well as put on plays for friends and family. Because the platform is movable, it can be placed in front of a small child's bed for safety at bedtime.

▦ Put a nightlight in the bedroom and keep the door ajar so your child never has to be frightened of the dark.

▦ Take your son or daughter to the store to select sheets for his or her bed. Long after the children are grown up, these sheets will hold special memories and can be treasured by future generations.

▦ Hang a display shelf on adjustable standards with brackets to house your child's personal treasures.

▦ After the crib stage, buy your child a *real* bed—not a junior one—that can last through adolescence and be dressed in a variety of styles throughout childhood.

▦ Lie on the floor in your child's room and look underneath the furniture to see what a little one sees.

▦ A bold graphic quilt on a wall is excellent decoration as well as stimulation for a child of any age. Attach it to the wall directly with self-adhesive Velcro tape or a lattice strip mounted to the wall with brads (headless nails).

▦ Set up a low table where your child can have a "tea party" with a friend.

▦ Together, paint some inexpensive oak chairs in bright primary colors. Let your child's imagination flow by encouraging yellow polka dots on grass green or tomato-red stripes alternating with white. Paint the child's name on the seat.

▦ Help your children arrange their books by subject matter or favorite authors so they will have a sense of ownership and pride in a growing library.

▦ Open shelves can hold a series of white Rubbermaid dishpans, which are ideal for clothes and toy storage. Tape a picture on the front end of each bin. Young children like to sort and match, and this trick also helps them put their toys back after playtime is over.

▦ Use a bright-colored beach pail for an accumulating crayon collection. Rather than using coloring books, supply blank sketch pads.

▦ Get down on the floor of this great room and play with your child.

Chapter 13

BATHROOMS

The bathroom greets us in the morning and helps us to wind down at night; and if it is a space that is easy on the eye as well as functional, we will find emotional and physical comfort from our time spent there. I am always refreshed by water, but I don't bathe just to get clean. I like to take a soak in the tub to meditate and cool off or simply to be left alone to daydream and think about special things I don't want to share with others in conversation.

In fact, time spent in a big, modern, expensive bathroom couldn't give me any more satisfaction than a peaceful moment in our simple Stonington haven, with its generous window overlooking the harbor. There are those who will disagree with me on this, but to my mind, bathroom renovations sometimes have a way of stripping away the charm and integrity of the space in order to make it architecturally "clean." Steam showers, Jacuzzis-for-two, and sunken marble tubs *can* be wonderful, but custom bathrooms are frightfully expensive to create. I have found that with bathrooms, just as with kitchens, you can often work with elements that already exist and still make functional changes that add to your comfort and convenience *without* going through a complete overhaul.

Given the funky nature of our house's design, it may not surprise you to learn that our so-called master bath is at the *end* of the upstairs hall! It startled us at first, but we have come to value it as a blessed grace note for our sense of privacy. Like the rest of the house, it had been in a rather decrepit state, and so we set to work at once, tiling the floor, replastering the cracked walls, and replacing the sink with one on a gleaming white pedestal, which we raised 2 inches by inserting a wooden block at the base, like a plinth at the bottom of a column. Painting the plinth high-gloss white makes it look like porcelain and it blends in beautifully with the white tile floor. Peter and I are both tall, and this small modification allows us to stand up straight when we brush our teeth.

Each bathroom imposes its own limitations because of space restrictions and preexisting plumbing, but we can make changes to increase our pleasure. By reevaluating your individual needs, you may discover you can make a minor alteration that will allow you to add another sink or a stall shower. One of my favorite master bathrooms is in an apartment that had a second bathroom door opening up into the study. By removing the door frame and putting wallboard on the study wall, the clients were able to create beautiful white double sinks set in a tiled vanity of intense cobalt blue. And in another apartment, where the bathroom dimensions were especially diminutive, we moved the sink into the corner, and had a mirrored medicine cabinet made to fit, which immediately improved the room's look.

When you have the luxury of space and an ample budget, there's no reason why you can't go for it. This is exactly what some clients did in their awesome bathroom. By removing a wall and taking out some closets, they made an elegant spa with an extra-large bathtub and whirlpool and mirrored walls. Friends also created a magnificent bath-and-exercise suite of gray granite, while other clients captured an extra couple of feet of space from an adjacent second bedroom. Their combination bath and dress-

Taste merely becomes a substitute for understanding and pleasure.
—Russell Lynes

ing area is done in white and pale pink tile, with pretty striped balloon shades hung at the windows to complement the pastel-striped wool carpet of the dressing area and hand-painted faux-marble cabinets, vanity, and closet doors.

Compared to these spaces, the bathroom in our Stonington house is extraordinarily humble! There is no light fixture over the mirror, for example, and there never was. So we put in a huge hinged mirror to enlarge the feeling of the room and to magnify the daylight. We can swing part of the mirror toward the light when Peter shaves, or when I'm applying makeup. The walls, with their high batten-board wainscoting, are painted white, and the ceiling is done in a soft blue. When I'm lying in the tub—the original one, which was voluptuously deep and which we had reenameled—I can look up contentedly at the skylike ceiling or past the window to the real sky outside. While I enjoy taking late-evening baths by the flickering light of a votive candle, we needed a ceiling fixture. But because the 7-foot ceiling is low, we couldn't accommodate one that hung down more than a few inches. Therefore, we selected an inexpensive white plastic fixture that we call "The Skylight," as that is what it looks like. It is clean and unobtrusive, giving off incandescent light through Lumiline tubes. When you're relaxing in the serenity of a soothing bath, you don't want to look up to see the harshness of an exposed light bulb.

Storage space is always at a premium in bathrooms, and so you may want to bring in a pretty painted chest in which to store medicines, cosmetics, shaving gear, and hair dryers during the day. Fortunately, behind our toilet there are two generous cupboards and behind the hinged mirror at the sink are shelves. Adjacent to the window are a couple of simple ledges, on which I have placed some pretty glass perfume bottles and jars with silver tops to house cotton balls, Q-Tips, and creams. We were also able to squeeze into the room a two-tiered wicker table, which we stack high with a changing array of fluffy pastel ter-

The most important functions of a building are its human uses.
—André Dubus

rycloth towels. In the winter, when we draw the water for a bath, I like to put our bath towels on top of the exposed white radiator so they're toasty warm and ready for us later.

With very little effort and not much expense, we turned a very ordinary bathroom into a nice place to spend private time. When you start to focus on your own bathrooms, your first observation may very well be that they aren't large enough. They never are. So you'll want to visually extend your walls and ceilings, as well as to keep all that porcelain equipment and wall tile at arm's length, by creating a light and uncluttered space.

In the bathroom, especially when we're in the tub, we often have time to look around the immediate environment without distractions. We notice dirt in the corners and cracks in the tiles, the spiderweb near the windowpane, and the peeling paint and stained wallpaper curling at the seams. So if you are planning to paint your bathroom, take time to lie down in your tub and look underneath the windowsill. If you have a mirror, it will reflect the door trim on the opposite wall. Be sure the entire edge is brightly painted also, including the top of the door trim that you think no one may notice. You will, and you'll wish you could turn water to paint long enough to dab a little trim color on those overlooked spots.

Because water is an essential aspect of all bathroom functions, you'll want to have waterproof walls and ceilings. Choose a wall covering that can be splashed and not become spoiled by moisture and steam. Because steam rises, the ceiling gets badly abused. A high-quality enamel paint might be a better bet than wall vinyl; and wall vinyl is best left to the powder room, where you don't have to worry about the glue opening up because of steam from the shower or tub. Remember, also, to consider the room's dimensions carefully when selecting wall and ceiling treatments. Like those of the kitchen, bathroom walls are generally partly covered with tile. Again, look for a simple, unified solution.

My clients often tell me that their greatest objections to their bathrooms, in addition to small size, is the tilework, which always seems to be in some truly unacceptable color. It is expensive to retile a bathroom, but if you do, consider using a couple of hand-glazed or -painted tiles, as discussed in the kitchen chapter; and allow for breakage during installation by purchasing 10 percent more tiles than you think you'll need. But if your tiles are old or are in poor condition, or if you do hate their color and can't afford to replace them, don't worry—enamel paint works just fine on tiles.

I love tile on a bathroom floor. Wall-to-wall carpeting strikes me as unnecessary *and* unsanitary. Area rugs, on the other hand, may be changed whenever you want *and* can be thrown into the washing machine. We enjoy using a variety of solid or patterned rugs in our bathroom; they infuse the room with splashes of color and create interest. Check your area rugs after every washing to be sure they've retained their elasticized bottoms. The dryer has a way of chewing those up, so now we let our rugs air-dry. The last thing you want when entering the bathroom is to take a fall.

To spruce up your bathroom, little things mean a lot. A sink or tub can be reenameled so that it sparkles again. A new attractive vanity can be installed and an ugly towel bar replaced. A beautiful shower curtain not only can coordinate with your bath mat or rug, it also conceals laundry racks. Look into the purchase of a super shower nozzle or hand-held shower attachment for massaging a sore muscle and rinsing shampoo out of your hair. This is a relaxing way to extend your bath pleasure and turn it into a mini-spa. We have an old-fashioned–looking brass faucet set that warms up the room and makes it glow.

I am, in fact, very much in my own world when in the bathroom. Everything I look at is soft, light, and harmonious. This intimate room is full of small luxuries—bath oils, soaps, a good drinking glass, a bud vase, a pretty, wall-mounted soap dish, magazines, and pictures—as yours should be: No room is too small to surround yourself with the accessories that turn daily routine into a celebration of pleasure. In this room, where you

Never underestimate common sense.

spend time each day, you need very few things, but they should be special and satisfying.

GRACE NOTES

▦ I encourage my clients to select all-white appliances. The deeper the color, the more the dirt shows.

▦ If you are tall, raise the height of the sink counter to approximately 34 inches.

▦ If you have a bathtub without a shower, you can install a combination of decorative tiles and mirror. Surround the three sides of the tub with four to five rows of 4-inch glazed tiles of azure blue, seafoam green, or white. One side of each tile is fully glazed, which should be installed on the front edge that shows. Above the tiles, install mirror panels on the three walls.

▦ Select clear Lucite towel bars with simple brass brackets.

▦ Select a tall brass goosenecked tub and sink faucet on a swivel.

▦ Towels help set the color scheme. In my daughters' blue and white bathroom, the towels are bright blue. The walls are white tiles with hand-painted blue clover leaves. When you limit the colors in the bathroom, the effect is very striking.

▦ Twelve-inch white ceramic floor tiles are ideal for almost every bathroom because they're easy to clean, don't discolor, and can be livened up with colorful area rugs.

⊞ Don't hide away all your colorful towels in the linen closet. Keep a generous stack of terrycloth towels and washcloths on a low, small white wicker table.

⊞ For everyday use, a selection of kitchen towels folded and rolled in a basket on the sink counter is colorful and practical. Unlike most cotton hand towels, they won't require ironing.

⊞ A basket with favorite soaps, bath salts, lotions, and powders is nice to have next to the tub.

⊞ Recessed ceiling lights are ideal to illuminate a bathroom evenly.

⊞ It's important when you're luxuriating in a deep tub, that you can look out at a beautiful view but no one can really see you. If you're overly concerned about privacy, turn out the lights and use a candle while you have a good soak.

⊞ Rather than having a separate sink unit, get a carpenter to build a cantilevered ledge out of plywood, which you can line with 4- to 5-inch tiles. Install an over-the-counter white porcelain oval sink approximately 12 by 20 inches.

⊞ If your bathroom needs renovation and you want an old-fashioned 20-inch-deep porcelain tub, house-wrecking and salvage businesses carry them. The outside of this tub can be painted any color with regular high-gloss oil paint. If the tub itself requires resurfacing, it can be sprayed with a special epoxy porcelain paint.

⊞ Frame a mirror behind the sink with a border of 5-inch tiles.

⊞ In white or lightly colored spaces, use graceful brass goose-necked faucet handles. With dark blue bathroom tiles, chrome-plated fixtures are attractive. The advantages are that they don't need polishing, can look as refreshing as silver, and are highly reflective.

⌗ If your view is not attractive, hang a bright, puffy-cloud shade above the window to draw attention away from what you see beyond.

⌗ A mirrored wall can actually be two large medicine cabinets on either side of a stationary center panel. Having the right-hand panel hinge on the left side, and the left-hand panel hinge on the right side lets the two mirrored wings act as a makeup mirror. Makeup lights on chrome or brass strips can be installed on either side of the mirrored wall.

⌗ Everything visible should be appealing to the eye. Blow dry-ers, electric curlers, shavers, Water Piks, and electric tooth-brushes should be stowed away after use. All these necessities can go in a wicker hinged storage table.

⌗ Install a pair of swing-arm lamps on either side of the mir-rored sink wall.

⌗ If your bathroom door hinges into the room, blocking the view of the window when the door is open, rehinge the door so that it opens into the next room. This way you can enjoy the light and view from the bathroom window from the connecting room. Some bathrooms are designed so well they are also a re-freshing sight.

⌗ If you need to do some work on your plumbing, rethink the location of the toilet. Place it so that it isn't visible when the door is open.

※ Hang a few narrow 5-inch-deep shelves on one wall to display pretty perfume bottles and small pictures and family photographs, as well as objects you adore.

※ Hang an old-fashioned brass rack for soap and sponges over the edge of the tub.

※ Rather than having a shower door over the tub, consider installing a clear glass baffle next to the shower head, 24 to 30 inches wide, trimmed in brass or chrome, so that you can shower and not feel caged in. A brass or chrome piano hinge allows the baffle to swing out into the room and rest against a wall when you're using the tub and want an open feeling.

※ If you are building a stall shower, pitch the drain so the water drains well. I seldom install a shower door for clients because it is not necessary when the shower head is accurately placed. Even if you have a shower head over a tub, you might not need a curtain, which makes you feel closed in.

※ Steam and water make bathroom wallpaper impractical. Some of my favorite bathrooms are all tiled. If you work with a plumber and do the tiling yourself, it cuts the cost way down and it lasts forever. I love tiles and find setting them enormously satisfying. In order to eliminate unnecessary cutting, measure your wall space and do a sketch, laying out each score (row) of tiles. Often, you can make the tiles come out evenly spaced by dividing up the number of tiles, minus the grouting.

※ Buy a hand-held shower attachment so you can have the luxury of soaking in a deep tub and washing your hair in comfort.

※ Paint clouds on the ceiling so you can look up from the bath and feel you're outside. First paint the ceiling Atmosphere Blue,

Fuller O'Brien 1-D-47, then sponge on puffy clouds in white-enamel semi-gloss. Add small touches of yellow and pink.

▨ Bathrooms have seasons also. Change the color scheme by changing your towels, bath mat, and area rugs.

▨ Simple white tab curtains on a white 1-inch wooden dowel are crisp, afford privacy, and don't block out too much light. Hang café curtains and close only the bottom pair.

▨ The bathroom in our New York apartment is small. Our emerald-green tiled counter ledge is held up by clear Plexiglas legs with brass caps and feet that don't take up any volume and are attractive. We enjoy having a bud vase on the counter and a few pretty jars and bottles. By mirroring the walls, we have magnified the space. Because everything in the bathroom is doubled by the mirror, we have to strictly edit what we put in there so that it doesn't look too cluttered.

▨ Let your bathroom be your retreat. Water is the rejuvenescence of the spirit.

Chapter 14

EXTERIORS

$\mathcal{J}$ purposely waited to discuss the outside of our house until close to the end of this book. Outer appearances, no matter how graceful, can never cover up for the absence of the soul and heart that must reside deep inside the interior spaces. The exterior of your house makes a statement to your neighbors, but that is all. It doesn't convey your happiness, your sense of joy in living inside, or your sense of personal style.

When we bought our dear house, it had been painted a muddy brown that some people refer to as taupe. The doors and trim were blue-green gray. There were some lonely azaleas that bloomed in May, but there was no grass, there were no shutters on the windows, and the entire property looked run-down and forlorn. I was able to see through all this emotionally, but not literally. I could see the possibilities of transformation beneath the depressing camouflage of neglect and decline. But to be honest, this was like the first house you drew in kindergarten — and we wanted to bring it back.

The last shall be first and the first shall be last. We began to show our care by putting in a new furnace and boiler. Then came the plumbing and the electricity. We scraped and sanded and stripped and painted to exorcise all the heavy, depressing colors

To conform within rational limits to a given style is no more servile than to pay one's taxes or to write according to the rules of grammar.
—Elsie de Wolfe

inside, and out. Just before we completed our second year of ownership, when our second spring came around, we had finished attacking the inside of the house, and were ready to begin resculpting it.

First, we installed a large antique sunburst window in the attic, replacing an awkward double-hung one. As we covered the once-brown exterior with white paint, we noticed the house growing in size and appearance. It seemed to stand up straight. We added some bottle-green shutters that have a touch of blue-black in their tone, which frame the windows in a symmetrical way, lending character where there had been blandness. The shutters punctuate the architectural lines and make the bright, white clapboard seem to have an inner glow, a radiance like a warm smile.

After all those years of apartment living, another of my life-long fantasies was to have *real* window boxes, brimming with a variety of pink geraniums. While the back of the house still needs major work, we now have window boxes in front and on two sides, a necklace that celebrates our house with the sublime beauty and color of flowers. A blanket of sod was rolled like a Turkish carpet in front, down the sides, and in the backyard, giving us the green grass those of us who live in urban spaces are starved for.

We added a white picket fence and two curved picket gates as a dazzling contrast to the bright green grass, which also defines our tiny property, only one seventh of an acre. Village life is not without nostalgia, especially given our town's long and dignified history; and so we put up a flagpole and hung a 1775 "Liberty and Union" flag, purchased from a regional museum. This was the flag used by the colonists in their revolt against England one year before the signing of the Declaration of Independence. Somehow, it felt right to us.

The crowning glory of the house is our beautiful Connecticut Valley door frame, which we actually spotted on the cover of an antiques show catalog in Colorado, where Peter and I had been lecturing. Peter was able to locate the dealer, and the proportions

Taste is our personal delight, our private dilemma, and our public facade.
—Russell Lynes,
The Tastemakers

and deep, magnificent carving of this door frame moved us both greatly. Over the phone, we reviewed the dimensions with our contractor, who gave us the green light to have it crated and shipped back to Connecticut. The door frame had returned to its original regional home.

The transformation of our house was magical, and was accomplished without undertaking major architectural work. All we did was add architectural detail—but the exterior facade was left essentially undisturbed.

You may have good reason to employ the services of a licensed architect, but there is a great deal that you can do to add aesthetic grace, character, and charm to your home without great fuss or expense. While Peter and I did not fix up the outside of our house to impress our neighbors, we did recognize that it would please them, and that is a deeply satisfying sensation. Recognition is a powerful human need; but more important, it simply feels good to know that you have done your part to add beauty to the environment at the same time you are pleasing yourself.

Ideas come from many places. I enjoy taking photographs of attractive houses whenever I travel, which has helped train my eye. Not long ago, we were visiting friends in Charleston, South Carolina, and touring its historic district. I snapped many pictures that day, and later when I studied the developed film, the fluted Doric columns of one of the front doors I liked suddenly presented itself as the right solution for a client I was helping. But then I was happy to let her architect take over.

We can make simple improvements to our homes by using color. White houses are gracious, but one of the most noticed buildings in our village is a strong periwinkle-blue house with an orange door, diagonally across the street from us. I love it, and the blue color of this house complements ours and intensifies its whiteness and light. There are professionals today called "color coordinators," who help their clients literally color-style the exteriors of their homes by using complementary (or contrasting) tones for trim, moldings, windows, shutters, and fa-

I've done just about all I can with what I've been given on earth.
—Eleanor McMillen Brown

cades. Of course, you can make good choices on your own, which can be as original or sedate as you wish.

Where once climate, local tradition, and the availability of building materials severely circumscribed the appearances of our houses, we can do almost anything today. A new brick house can be made to look weathered and mellow by whitewashing the brick. The thin coat of white paint eventually sloughs off to expose the brick in a mellow tone. Slate or cedar shake roofs are expensive to install, but synthetic versions give the same appearance and won't break the bank. If you travel through the South, you may observe how many of its first plantation houses had architectural embellishments added on to them after their owners became more prosperous. A plain front porch could take on the appearance of a Greek temple with classical Ionic, Doric, or Corinthian columns.

We, too, can graft on to our houses elements that attract us, much as those southern plantation owners did. You can add premade pediments, columns, pilasters, fan windows, and architectural gingerbread; or French doors, shutters, porches, terraces, or decks. The exterior finish can be aluminum, clapboard or cedar siding, brick, stone, or stucco; and dormer, muntin, or picture windows can be added. You can alter the roof line or change the roofing material to make it look more dramatic. Roofing material comes in a wide variety of colors: Some friends replaced the dark brown roof of their Pennsylvania stone house with one that's crimson red. Suddenly, this old house came alive.

There is no longer any reason to hide your light under a bushel. Consider what you can do to flatter your house. Your schemes may be as simple as resurfacing a driveway or walkway with gravel, slate, brick, or stone; planting new shrubbery or flowerbeds; putting on a fresh coat of paint or putting up new shutters; or creating a new entrance. You can add new front steps, window boxes, a trellis, a veranda, or a porte cochere. A fence, wall, or gate can provide character as well as privacy. A

The roses are a bit over their prime.
—Eleanor McMillen Brown

new mailbox, lamppost, house number sign, piece of sculpture, gazebo, awnings, or exterior lights can make a world of difference. Big things make a big difference, but so do little things.

I love the way the exterior of our house looks and feels. Peter, who has really come to love that flagpole, enjoys choosing a different flag every day. We're planning to create a walled garden in the back next summer. We'll put mirror behind the white trellis so it will sparkle and reflect light, and the ivy we've planted will hug it. For now, we love seeing pink impatiens from our kitchen windows. When our front gates are closed and latched, we can leave the front door open to flood the house with sea air and light. In the evenings, we often sit in our doorway, which is ideal for two, lean back against it, and watch people walking by. We can see the boats returning to the harbor for the evening. We decided against having a lantern, since the lights inside the house give a warm, pink, cozy glow.

Having restored the outside of our home makes us happy. The pure architectural bones have integrity. We removed anything that wasn't straightforward. The simplicity of white contrasted with the green grass and bottle-green shutters is strong and handsome. The geraniums add color and life.

I am often asked if I design houses from the inside out or from the outside in. Clearly, I believe architecture should be alive and flexible enough to incorporate our dreams and needs inside—but we should never become slaves to external appearances. It is true, however, that when you spend two years working on a house, often doing things no one will ever see, and then you restore the exterior, you can take pride in your accomplishments. The exterior is the picture you paint for your neighbors, your community, and the world that passes by. The outside will never have the same intimacy as the inside, but the architecture and yard can express your personality, your appreciation of beauty and life, and your love of home.

Home is a combination of human will and divine grace.

GRACE NOTES

⊞   Houses have four sides. View your house from all angles. Depending on where you view it, it will show distinctly different characteristics.

⊞   If your curtains show from the exterior, check that the linings are always cheerful and clean.

⊞   Build wooden window boxes the width of the windows all around the first floor of your house. Drill two holes on the bottom of each window box, one on each end, for drainage. Plant the front and two sides of the house with flowers. The back of the house can have a variety of flowering plants to coordinate with your secret garden, out of sight from the road.

⊞   I'm from New England and love white houses. Install deep bottle-green shutters on all the windows. Measure the height of each window and use unpainted shutters from the lumberyard.

⊞   Spray-paint the shutters out-of-doors over drop cloths with Shaded Spruce, Fuller O'Brien 1-E-130. Spray one shutter and use it as a sample over several days to make sure the color is pleasing during different times of day or at night.

⊞   Before investing in expensive outside lanterns, consider having the house lit from the inside only. Perhaps you could have just a small light to illuminate the front door.

⊞   Hang a brass or copper bracket on the front of the house to hold a flagpole. The American Flag Company in New York City offers a wide assortment of poles (and accepts telephone orders). They also sell flags.

▦ "Good fences make good neighbors." The fence you select should be in keeping with the mood of your house. What would be best for the house? Stone, white picket, or split rail? Do you feel it should be a white fence or be stained brown? Do not substitute plastic for painted wood.

▦ In the privacy of your backyard, consider having a green and white striped canvas awning to shade your flagstone terrace or wooden deck.

▦ If you are building a deck behind your house, do not remove the trees, but incorporate them into the deck by cutting around them. To take the raw orange tone out of redwood, use Cabot's bleaching oil, which will weather the deck to a silver tone in weeks.

▦ Look in magazines and garden books for inspiration for a variety of different possible trellis designs to incorporate into your deck and garden wall.

▦ When planning a trellis wall, install sheets of mirror behind it so that when ivy and other plants are fully grown, the mirror will expand your garden and illuminate it with a sunny glow even in a shaded area.

▦ Select the design and color of outdoor furniture to coordinate with the style and character of your house. For a stone Tudor-style house, you may choose iron filigree furniture, but if your house has a contemporary feeling, keep the furniture light with simple lines.

▦ On either side of the steps leading to your front door, have a variety of large terra-cotta pots brimming with geraniums, pansies, or other flowers.

✳ Look at your front door. Can you improve on the hardware? Doorknob, knocker, and mail slot? A nice touch is to have a sliding brass oval cover to hide the keyhole.

✳ If you are contemplating changing the roofing material to slate or cedar shakes, check first with the local building department for your community's weight and fire regulations.

✳ When you uplift the appearance of the exterior of your house, it will beckon you to go outside and enjoy nature touching your home.

Chapter 15

LIVING AT HOME

L ife isn't fair. There's no question that some people have a greater capacity to live more fully than others. In my time, I've made thousands of house calls, and I've been privileged to see, firsthand, how thousands of families really live at home. When you observe the appearance, the spirit, mood, and vitality of a house, you get an honest feeling for the chemistry of the people who dwell in it. When people create a beautiful home, it can be felt and understood immediately.

A physical shelter, no matter how grand or humble, cannot come to life on its own. A house is people-made. And when those people address it with an appreciation for the beauty around them and are inspired to create more beauty, they will be the fortunate ones whose homes will be brimming with love.

Houses speak your language. Rooms take on your sensitivity, mood, attitude, and spirit. And when you are feeling discouraged, your four walls will comfort you because they will reflect back on you, remind you of your energy and personality. A house becomes your friend; the furniture, your possessions, your most intimate circle.

The French Regency fruitwood carved table with a marble top I bought for less than three hundred dollars thirty years ago

A home is what you make it.
— Jennifer Byrd

is no longer a piece of furniture. I've written ten books at this table; I've said grace, given toasts, broken bread, dined with family and dear friends, and nourished them with the food I prepared. The fact that the table is now worth thousands of dollars is irrelevant. No one in my family would ever sell this table, because it would be like selling my soul.

The love that is felt and shared in a house attaches itself to the air you breathe. You feel the vibrations of the occupants, you sense the values and vitality of the individual personalities, and their dreams, fantasies, and disappointments. It celebrates what you love, empathizing with what you've lost, and focuses on what is authentic. But if we are caught up too fiercely in the day-to-day routine of chores, duties, and coping, we may never create a beautiful home. A home is not a constant work trap where everything is done to rigid schedule so that we can cross things off that we've accomplished on our "To Do" pads, in fear, exhaustion, or discouragement that we can never get caught up or finished. We shouldn't value efficiency and regime over serendipity and grace. If we can't unwind and curl up with a good book by a crackling warm fire just because there's work we should do, we are missing it all. The dishes won't walk away, but the moment may.

Similarly, when we become more conscious about how our house looks than how it feels, we will wonder what eludes us, why it is we don't feel better at home. People have often told me that they thought that once they "decorated" their house, then everything would fall into place. But that's not how life works: We can finish a house, but never a home. Once you fall in love with a house, you find continual pleasures in fixing it up and making innovations that satisfy your creature comforts. Everywhere else in your life you may live by the schedules and timetables of others. You don't own those moments. They are not yours; you cannot control them. But at home you can live fully in those moments because they belong to you.

It is in the creation of a beautiful home that you leave your

Cultivate the habit of attention at home.

mark, in this place that envelops your mind, body, and soul. It is the center of your life circle. A house responds to you reflexively, giving back more than you could ever put in to it. If you are a grumpy person and treat where you live in a perfunctory way, that is what your house will give back to you. If you decorate in a frenzy so you can get it all behind you before you can begin to live, you may find yourself on a stage that is set for the wrong play. Decorating is a process that should continue throughout your lifetime. Don't think of decorating, think of creating.

Houses have to be loved and appreciated in order for them to grow naturally. Now you are on your own. You've got all the tools you need to create your own magical environments. It will be hard work, but joyful and fulfilling. I hope you will be moved to share your experiences with me, as I have with you. For it is my most fervent wish that for us both, creating a beautiful home can be our life's crowning achievement, delighting and satisfying us all the way in the process.

Home has finally become a real refuge of comfort and peace.

My Acknowledgment, with Appreciation

THE BIRTH OF THE HOUSE BOOK

The process of this book has been a labor and journey of love. As the book is complete, I'm filled with mixed emotions. Great happiness, I've discovered, comes from working on something you believe in, working with talented, enthusiastic people. Every stage has been intensely exciting. While there is a sense of relief that the book is finished, ready to be printed, there is a touch of sadness that, with completion, we will not have the same sense of accomplishment. But we can all look forward to seeing the bound book, each of us knowing how much fun it has been working together.

Books are created by a team. We are all interconnected, linking together to create something synergistically bigger than any of us individually. I'm grateful to have been guided by great, talented editors—brilliant artists responsible for shaping my work. My first editor, Kate Medina, at Doubleday and later Random House, thank you for enhancing my voice, guiding the growth of my work, and stretching my vision. Sally Arteseros, who took over as my editor at Doubleday during a vital, productive time, thank you for the depth you bring to my thinking and your tenderness in encouraging my communication. Together, you two have given me a library of my books, which gives me pleasure and has opened up a world of rich, treasured, shared memories.

Marysarah Quinn, working with you on this book eases the bumps of change, provides continuity, assures a more beautiful book and brings me great joy. Thanks, Babe.

Carl Brandt, all this love and enjoyment in the process is due to you. I value every bit of advice you give me. When you speak, I listen. You've taught me that there is only one point of view, the big picture. Thank you for being the pillar.

Peter, I love you. Because I write in bed as well as in my Zen room, side by side, you've been right here, sharing in the fun. Thanks for inventing solitude for two with "writer's workshop." The book is alive because you and I live with such happiness here in my first house, our home.

Lisel Eisenheimer, my friend and editor at *McCall's*. I thank you for all the laughter as we met our column deadlines. Your wise counsel, our great conversations, your ideas and talent I look up to and value as lasting gifts.

I thank the editor-in-chief of *McCall's*, Kate White. Not only did you publish pictures of the house, but you continue to encourage me to use the house, our home, as the backbone of my *McCall's* column. I appreciate being able to share my excitement each month with your readers.

Ellen Edwards, my Avon editor, I thank you for your belief in me, your guidance and caring, as well as your ideas for books which are wise and wonderful.

Special appreciation to Amy Belleau, a talented writer whom I met at *McCall's*, who offered to put my fuchsia longhand writing on a computer and print it out for my editor. Our visits, our Federal Express dates, our deadlines, our conversations make me aware of your dedication to my published work.

ACKNOWLEDGMENTS

Elisabeth Carey Lewis, you are the best! I love working with you every day and appreciate your help in *all* our projects.

Over these twenty-five years of writing for publication, I've met hundreds of people I think of often with great respect and appreciation: Carolyn Reidy, Mark Gompertz, Louis Oliver Gropp, Fred Weidner, Barbara Donovan Tober, D. J. Carey, Patricia Corbin, Claire Whitcomb, Tish Baldridge, Alex Gotfryd, Bob Aulicino, Bob O'Brien, thanks.

To all my interns who have dreamed up Grace Notes, done research, taken pictures, cut and pasted, worked on book tours, I thank each of you and am proud of you. "Good stuff," Dinah Moore.

Stephen Freeburg, thanks for coming up to stay at the house to get a feeling for its spirit. Your artwork captures the essence of home.

Alexandra, thanks for falling in love with our village and gently persuading me that it was time for Mom to have her first house.

Brooke, my stylist, thanks for our shop talk, for your excellent ideas and all our collaborations here and in France.

To my brilliant editor Susan Leon, I thank you for your dedication to my book. You made it your mission too. Through your honing, your moving around of material, your reading my other work and getting inside my voice, you've smoothed out the writing so that it sounds like the *real* song. What poured out of me like hot lava is now my favorite book. I appreciate you and the whole team.

Sincere thanks to my readers who have taken the time to write me wonderful letters, encouraging me to continue to create.

Alexandra Stoddard

Stonington Village
July 24, 1992